NOVA SCOTIA TRAVEL GUIDE

Discover the Untouched Beauty of Nova Scotia: Your Ticket to Adventure and Relaxation

Chris West

All rights reserved. No part of this book may be reproduced, stored in a retrieval system, or transmitted in any form or by any means, electronic, mechanical, photocopying, recording, or otherwise, without the prior written permission of the copyright owner. The information contained in this book is for general information purposes only. The author and publisher make no representations or warranties of any kind, express or implied, about the completeness, accuracy, reliability, suitability or availability with respect to the book or the information, products, services, or related graphics contained in the book for any purpose. Any reliance you place on such information is therefore strictly at your own risk.

Copyright © 2023 by Chris West.

TABLE OF CONTENT

Introduction
- Welcome to Nova Scotia
- Why visit Nova Scotia
- When to visit Nova Scotia
- How Long to Stay
- Budgeting and Money Matters
- Accommodation Options

Chapter 2: Planning Your Trip
- Getting to Nova Scotia
- Getting around Nova Scotia
- Where to stay in Nova Scotia
- Nova Scotia Travel Iteneraries

Chapter 3: Halifax and Surrounding Areas
- Overview of Halifax
- Why Visit Halifax?
- Things to see and do in Halifax
  - Historic Halifax Citadel National Historic Site
  - Maritime Museum of the Atlantic
  - Halifax Public Gardens
  - Halifax Waterfront Boardwalk
  - Art Gallery of Nova Scotia
  - Halifax Central Library
  - Canadian Museum of Immigration
  - Halifax Seaport Farmers' Market
- Day trips from Halifax

Chapter 4: South Shore and Annapolis Valley
- Overview of the South Shore and Annapolis Valley

Things to see and do in the South Shore and Annapolis Valley

Day trips from the South Shore and Annapolis Valley

Where to eat in the South Shore and Annapolis Valley

Chapter 5: Cape Breton Island

Overview of Cape Breton Island

Things to see and do in Cape Breton Island

Day trips from Cape Breton Island

Where to eat in Cape Breton Island

Chapter 6: Northumberland Shore and Eastern Shore

Overview of the Northumberland Shore and Eastern Shore

Things to see and do in the Northumberland Shore and Eastern Shore

Day trips from the Northumberland Shore and Eastern Shore

Where to eat in the Northumberland Shore and Eastern Shore

Chapter 7: Outdoor Adventures in Nova Scotia

Hiking and walking trails

Beaches and water activities

Whale watching and wildlife tours

Golf courses and skiing

Chapter 8: Nova Scotia's Cultural Scene

Museums and historic sites

Festivals and events
Performing arts and music
Art galleries and studios
Chapter 9: Practical Information
Nova Scotia's history and culture
Money and costs
Payment options and credit cards
Tipping etiquette
  Health and safety
Language and communication
Useful apps and websites
Conclusion

Introduction

Welcome to Nova Scotia

Nova Scotia is a province located on the eastern coast of Canada, bordered by the Atlantic Ocean to the east and New Brunswick to the west. With a population of around one million people, Nova Scotia is a relatively small province known for its stunning natural scenery, rich history and culture, and friendly locals.

Nova Scotia has a long and diverse history that dates back thousands of years to its Indigenous roots. The province was also an important hub for European exploration and colonization, with a rich and complex history that is evident in its architecture, museums, and cultural heritage sites.

Today, Nova Scotia is a thriving travel destination that offers something for everyone, whether you're interested in exploring charming coastal towns, hiking in national parks, indulging in local cuisine, or attending cultural festivals and events.

The province is divided into several distinct regions, each with its own unique character and attractions. Halifax and the surrounding areas are the cultural and economic heart of the province, with a vibrant arts scene, historic landmarks, and picturesque waterfront.

The South Shore and Annapolis Valley are home to some of the province's most idyllic towns and villages, as well as stunning beaches, wineries, and hiking trails. Cape Breton Island, located in the northeastern part of the province, is renowned for its rugged coastline, Scottish heritage, and the famous Cabot Trail driving route.

The Northumberland Shore and Eastern Shore are quieter and more laid-back regions, with a focus on outdoor recreation, local crafts and cuisine, and maritime history.

Whether you're a first-time visitor or a seasoned traveler, Nova Scotia is a province that is sure to captivate and inspire you. With its breathtaking scenery, rich cultural heritage, and warm hospitality, Nova Scotia is a truly special place that is well worth exploring.

Why visit Nova Scotia

Natural Scenery:

Nova Scotia's natural beauty is one of its biggest draws. From the rugged coastline and picturesque fishing villages to the rolling hills and expansive forests, there is no shortage of stunning scenery to explore. Some of the top natural attractions in Nova Scotia include the Cabot Trail, Kejimkujik National Park, Peggy's Cove, and the Bay of Fundy.

Rich History and Culture:

Nova Scotia has a long and fascinating history that is reflected in its culture, traditions, and landmarks. Visitors can learn about the province's Indigenous roots, the arrival of European settlers, and its role in important historical events such as the American Revolution and World War II. There are also many cultural experiences to enjoy, such as visiting art galleries and museums, attending festivals and events, and sampling local cuisine.

Friendly Locals:

Nova Scotians are known for their warm and welcoming nature, and visitors can expect to be greeted with genuine hospitality throughout the province. Whether you're chatting with a local shopkeeper or striking up a conversation with a stranger in a pub, you're likely to find that Nova Scotians are happy to share their knowledge and experiences with visitors.

Outdoor Activities:

For outdoor enthusiasts, Nova Scotia is a paradise. There are countless opportunities for hiking, biking, kayaking, and other activities, with many trails and waterways offering stunning views and wildlife sightings. Whether you're an experienced adventurer or a beginner looking for a fun day trip, there are options for all skill levels.

Culinary Delights:

Nova Scotia's food scene is a reflection of its coastal location and agricultural heritage. Visitors can indulge in fresh seafood, locally sourced produce, and artisanal products such as craft beer and wine. Whether you're dining in a fine restaurant or grabbing a snack from a food truck, you're sure to find delicious and unique flavors to sample.

Festivals and Events:

Nova Scotia is home to a vibrant arts and culture scene, with numerous festivals and events taking place throughout the year. Some of the most popular include the Halifax International Busker Festival, the Celtic Colours International Festival, and the Halifax Jazz Festival. These events offer a chance to experience local music, dance, and other forms of entertainment in a fun and festive atmosphere.

Coastal Towns and Beaches:

Nova Scotia's coastline is dotted with charming towns and villages that offer a glimpse into the province's rich maritime history. From the bustling city of Halifax to the quaint fishing village of Lunenburg, there are countless picturesque towns to explore. In addition, Nova Scotia boasts some of the most beautiful beaches in Canada, with miles of sandy shoreline and crystal-clear waters.

Wildlife Watching:

Nova Scotia is home to a diverse array of wildlife, including whales, seals, eagles, and moose. Visitors can take a whale watching tour, go birdwatching, or explore the many hiking trails and parks where wildlife sightings are common. For nature lovers, Nova Scotia is a paradise.

Adventure Sports:

For those seeking a thrill, Nova Scotia offers plenty of options. Visitors can go ziplining, rock climbing, or even try their hand at surfing. With its rugged coastline, dense forests, and challenging terrain, Nova Scotia is a playground for adventure seekers.

Relaxation and Wellness:

For those looking to unwind, Nova Scotia offers many opportunities for relaxation and wellness. Visitors can take a yoga class, indulge in a spa treatment, or simply enjoy a peaceful walk along the beach. With its tranquil surroundings and laid-back atmosphere, Nova Scotia is the perfect destination for a stress-free getaway.

Nova Scotia offers a wealth of experiences for travelers of all interests and preferences. Whether you're looking to explore the great outdoors, immerse yourself in the local culture, or simply relax and unwind, Nova Scotia has something to offer.

When to visit Nova Scotia

Nova Scotia experiences four distinct seasons, each with its own unique charm. Here is a breakdown of what to expect during each season:

Spring (March - May):

- Spring is a time of renewal in Nova Scotia, as the snow melts away and the landscape begins to come back to life.
- Temperatures are mild, with average highs ranging from 5°C (41°F) in March to 18°C (64°F) in May.
- Spring is a great time to see wildflowers, migratory birds, and other wildlife in the province's parks and natural areas.

Summer (June - August):

- Summer is the peak tourist season in Nova Scotia, when the weather is warm and sunny and many popular attractions are open.
- Average highs range from 20°C (68°F) in June to 24°C (75°F) in August, with occasional heat waves.
- Summer is a great time to visit the province's beaches, go whale watching, attend festivals and events, and explore the outdoors.

Fall (September - November):

- Fall is a spectacular season in Nova Scotia, when the leaves on the trees turn brilliant shades of red, orange, and yellow.
- Temperatures begin to cool in September, with average highs ranging from 18°C (64°F) to 12°C (54°F) in November.
- Fall is a great time to go hiking, visit wineries and orchards, attend harvest festivals, and enjoy the province's stunning fall foliage.

Winter (December - February):

- Winter in Nova Scotia is cold and snowy, but also incredibly beautiful and peaceful.
- Average highs range from -1°C (30°F) in December to 0°C (32°F) in February, with occasional storms and blizzards.

- Winter is a great time to go skiing, snowshoeing, or skating, enjoy the holiday festivities, and cozy up by a warm fire in a cabin or inn.

Overall, the best time to visit Nova Scotia really depends on what you're interested in seeing and doing. Summer is the most popular season for tourists, but spring, fall, and even winter can be great times to visit for those who enjoy outdoor activities, cultural events, or a quieter pace of travel.

How Long to Stay

Nova Scotia is a beautiful province located on Canada's east coast. With its stunning scenery, rich history, and vibrant culture, it's no wonder that many visitors wonder how long they should stay when visiting. The answer to this question largely depends on your travel goals and interests, as well as your schedule and budget. we will explore some of the factors you should consider when deciding how long to stay in Nova Scotia.

Your Travel Goals and Interests

The first factor to consider when deciding how long to stay in Nova Scotia is your travel goals and interests. If you're looking to explore the province's natural beauty, you'll want to set aside more time to visit its national parks, hiking trails, and beaches. Similarly, if you're interested in learning about the province's history and culture, you may want to spend more time in its museums, galleries, and historic sites. On the other hand, if you're simply looking to relax and unwind, you may only need a few days to soak up Nova Scotia's laid-back vibe.

Distance and Transportation

Another factor to consider is how far you need to travel to get to Nova Scotia and how you plan to get around once you're there. If you're driving, you'll need to factor in the time it takes to get to the province, as well as the time it takes to drive between different destinations within Nova Scotia. If you're flying, you'll need to factor in the time it takes to get to the airport, go through security, and wait for your flight.

Once you're in Nova Scotia, you'll need to decide how you plan to get around. If you're renting a car, you'll have more flexibility to explore the province at your own pace. However, if you're relying on public transportation or organized tours, you may need to factor in more time to account for schedules and waiting times.

Seasonal Considerations

Nova Scotia's weather and seasonal events can also affect how long you should stay when visiting. If you're interested in outdoor activities like hiking, camping, or beach-going, you may want to visit in the summer when temperatures are warmer and the days are longer. Similarly, if you're interested in attending festivals or events like the Halifax Jazz Festival or the Halifax Busker Festival, you'll need to plan your visit around those dates.

On the other hand, if you're interested in winter sports like skiing or snowboarding, you may want to visit in the winter when the province's ski hills are open. However, keep in mind that winter weather can be unpredictable, and some attractions and activities may be closed or have reduced hours.

Budget

Finally, your budget will also play a role in determining how long you should stay in Nova Scotia. The province offers a range of accommodations, from budget-friendly hostels to luxury hotels, so there are options for every budget. However, the longer you stay, the more you'll need to budget for accommodations, food, transportation, and activities.

Here are some suggested itineraries for how long to stay in Nova Scotia based on different travel goals and interests:

Nature lovers: If you're interested in exploring Nova Scotia's natural beauty, you'll want to set aside at least 5-7 days to visit its national parks, hiking trails, and beaches. Consider spending a few days in Cape Breton Highlands National Park, where you can hike the Skyline Trail and explore the Cabot Trail scenic drive. Then, head south to the Kejimkujik National Park and Historic Site to paddle in its lakes and rivers and camp under the stars. Finish your trip by spending a day or two exploring the beaches and coastal towns along the South Shore.

History and culture buffs: If you're interested in learning about Nova Scotia's rich history and vibrant culture, you'll want to spend at least 3-5 days in the province. Start your trip in Halifax, where you can visit the Maritime Museum of the Atlantic, the Halifax Citadel National Historic Site, and the Art Gallery of Nova Scotia. Then, head to Lunenburg, a UNESCO World Heritage Site, to see its well-preserved 18th-century architecture and visit the Fisheries Museum of the Atlantic. Finally, head to Annapolis Royal to visit Fort Anne National Historic Site and learn about the province's Acadian and Mi'kmaq cultures.

Relaxation and unwinding: If you're looking to simply relax and unwind, you can still enjoy a peaceful and rejuvenating trip to Nova Scotia in just 2-3 days. Consider spending a day or two in the charming coastal town of Mahone Bay, where you can stroll along its picturesque waterfront and browse its artisan shops and galleries. Then, head to the nearby town of Lunenburg to sample its delicious seafood and take in its peaceful harbor views. Finish your trip by visiting the tranquil beaches of Lawrencetown or Martinique, where you can unwind in the sun and surf.

Food and drink enthusiasts: Nova Scotia is also known for its delicious food and drink, including fresh seafood, craft beer, and wine. If you're interested in indulging in Nova Scotia's culinary delights, you'll want to spend at least 3-5 days exploring the province's food and drink scene. Start your trip in Halifax, where you can sample local craft beer at the Garrison Brewing Company and taste the city's famous donair at King of Donair. Then, head to the Annapolis Valley to visit its wineries and cideries and enjoy a farm-to-table meal at one of its many restaurants. Finish your trip by exploring the fishing villages and seafood shacks along the South Shore, where you can feast on lobster, scallops, and fish and chips.

Overall, Nova Scotia offers a wide range of experiences for visitors of all interests and travel styles. By considering your travel goals, budget, and other factors, you can plan a trip that will allow you to make the most of your time in this beautiful province.

Budgeting and Money Matters

Nova Scotia is a beautiful province located on the east coast of Canada. It is known for its picturesque landscapes, rich culture, and welcoming people. However, like any travel destination, a trip to Nova Scotia can come with expenses that can quickly add up. In this article, we will discuss budgeting and money matters when visiting Nova Scotia to help you make the most of your trip without breaking the bank.

Plan your expenses

The first step to budgeting for a trip to Nova Scotia is to plan your expenses. Start by making a list of all the things you want to do, see, and experience while in Nova Scotia. This may include accommodation, transportation, food, activities, and souvenirs. Research the costs associated with each item and create a budget that aligns with your financial goals.

Book your accommodation in advance

One of the biggest expenses of any trip is accommodation. Booking your accommodation in advance can help you save money and stay within your budget. There are many options for accommodation in Nova Scotia, including hotels, motels, bed and breakfasts, and vacation rentals. Consider your budget and the location you want to stay in, and book your accommodation as early as possible to take advantage of any discounts or deals.

Use public transportation

Transportation costs can quickly add up, especially if you plan on renting a car. Consider using public transportation, such as buses and trains, to save money on transportation costs. Many cities in Nova Scotia have reliable public transportation systems, and taking public transportation can be an excellent way to see the sights while staying within your budget.

Take advantage of free activities

Nova Scotia is full of natural beauty and cultural experiences that don't require spending money. Take advantage of free activities such as hiking, visiting museums, and exploring local markets. Many cities and towns in Nova Scotia have free events throughout the year, such as festivals and concerts, so be sure to check local listings.

Eat local

Food is an essential part of any trip, and Nova Scotia is known for its delicious seafood and farm-fresh produce. Eating local can be a great way to save money and experience the local culture. Visit local farmers' markets, seafood shacks, and restaurants to sample local cuisine at a fraction of the cost of fine dining.

Purchase souvenirs wisely

Souvenirs can be a great way to remember your trip to Nova Scotia, but they can also be expensive. To stay within your budget, consider purchasing souvenirs wisely. Look for locally made products, such as art and crafts, that are unique to Nova Scotia. Avoid buying souvenirs in tourist areas, where prices are often inflated.

Be aware of fees and taxes

When budgeting for your trip to Nova Scotia, be aware of fees and taxes that may be added to your expenses. For example, many hotels and vacation rentals charge additional fees, such as cleaning fees or resort fees. Sales tax is also added to most purchases in Nova Scotia, so be sure to factor this into your budget.

In conclusion, budgeting for a trip to Nova Scotia is all about planning ahead and making smart financial decisions. By creating a budget, booking your accommodation in advance, using public transportation, taking advantage of free activities, eating local, purchasing souvenirs wisely, and being aware of fees and taxes, you can make the most of your trip to Nova Scotia without breaking the bank. Happy travels!

Accommodation Options

Nova Scotia, a province in eastern Canada, offers a variety of accommodation options for visitors. From cozy bed and breakfasts to luxurious hotels, visitors have a wide range of options to choose from depending on their budget and preferences. we'll explore some of the most popular accommodation options for visitors to Nova Scotia.

Hotels: Nova Scotia has a wide range of hotels to suit every budget and taste. From budget-friendly hotels like Comfort Inn and Best Western to luxurious properties like The Westin Nova Scotian and The Prince George Hotel, there are plenty of options to choose from. Some of these hotels are located in the heart of downtown Halifax, while others are situated in scenic locations such as Cape Breton Island.

Bed and Breakfasts: For those seeking a more personal and cozy experience, bed and breakfasts are a popular option in Nova Scotia. There are many charming B&Bs located throughout the province, offering a comfortable and intimate atmosphere. Many B&Bs offer homemade breakfasts and personalized service, making them a great choice for those looking for a home away from home.

Inns and Guesthouses: Inns and guesthouses are another great option for visitors to Nova Scotia. Many of these properties are located in historic buildings and offer a unique and charming experience. Inns and guesthouses can range from budget-friendly options to luxurious properties, offering something for everyone.

Vacation Rentals: Vacation rentals are a great option for those looking for more space and privacy. Nova Scotia has a wide range of vacation rentals, including cottages, apartments, and homes. Many vacation rentals are located in scenic locations such as along the coast or in the countryside, offering visitors a chance to experience the natural beauty of the province.

Campgrounds: For those looking for a more rustic experience, campgrounds are a popular option in Nova Scotia. The province has many campgrounds located throughout the province, offering visitors a chance to experience the great outdoors. Some campgrounds offer amenities such as showers, laundry facilities, and playgrounds, while others offer a more primitive experience.

In conclusion, Nova Scotia offers a wide range of accommodation options for visitors. Whether you're looking for a luxurious hotel or a cozy bed and breakfast, there are plenty of options to choose from. Whatever your budget and preferences, Nova Scotia has something to offer for everyone.

Chapter 2: Planning Your Trip

Getting to Nova Scotia

Nova Scotia is located on the east coast of Canada and is easily accessible by air, land, and sea. Here are some of the most popular ways to get to Nova Scotia:

By plane: Halifax Stanfield International Airport is the main airport in Nova Scotia and is served by several major airlines including Air Canada, WestJet, and Delta Airlines. The airport is located about 35 minutes from downtown Halifax and has direct flights to and from many major cities in Canada, the United States, and Europe.

By car: Nova Scotia is connected to the rest of Canada and the United States by several highways, including the Trans-Canada Highway and the Interstate 95. There are several border crossings between Nova Scotia and New Brunswick, Quebec, and Maine. Driving to Nova Scotia is a popular option for those who want to explore the province at their own pace.

By ferry: There are two ferry services that operate in Nova Scotia. The first is the CAT ferry, which runs between Yarmouth, Nova Scotia and Portland,

Maine during the summer months. The second is the Northumberland Ferries, which runs between Wood Islands, Prince Edward Island and Caribou, Nova Scotia year-round. Both ferry services provide a scenic way to travel to Nova Scotia and are popular with tourists.

Once you arrive in Nova Scotia, there are several transportation options to get around the province, including car rentals, public transportation, taxis, and ride-sharing services. It's important to plan your transportation in advance to ensure a smooth and hassle-free trip.

Overall, Nova Scotia is an easy-to-reach destination with a variety of transportation options to suit different needs and budgets. Whether you're flying in for a short weekend trip or driving in for an extended vacation, getting to Nova Scotia is the first step to an unforgettable adventure.

Getting around Nova Scotia

When it comes to getting around Nova Scotia, there are a variety of transportation options available, depending on your budget and preferences.

Car Rentals
Renting a car is a popular option for tourists visiting Nova Scotia. There are several car rental companies

to choose from, including international brands like Enterprise, Budget, and Hertz, as well as local companies like Discount Car and Truck Rentals and Rent-A-Wreck. You can pick up and drop off your car rental at various locations throughout the province, including Halifax Stanfield International Airport.

Public Transportation
If you're traveling on a budget, public transportation is a good option to consider. Halifax Transit operates a comprehensive bus network in the Halifax Regional Municipality, with fares ranging from $2.75 to $5.00 depending on the distance traveled. There are also regional bus services operated by companies like Acadian Lines and Maritime Bus, which connect Halifax with other cities and towns throughout Nova Scotia.

Taxis and Ride-Sharing Services
Taxis are widely available in Halifax and other urban areas, and you can usually find them at taxi stands or by calling a local taxi company. Uber and Lyft also operate in Halifax, although their availability may be limited in some areas.

Biking and Walking
Nova Scotia's scenic landscape is ideal for biking and walking, with many trails and paths available for recreational use. Halifax has an extensive network of bike lanes and multi-use trails, including

the popular Halifax Harbourwalk, which runs along the waterfront. You can rent bikes from several shops in Halifax, or bring your own and explore the province at your own pace.

Ferries
Ferries are another option for getting around Nova Scotia, particularly if you're traveling to or from the neighboring province of Prince Edward Island or the state of Maine in the United States. The Northumberland Ferries operates a seasonal ferry service between Caribou, Nova Scotia and Wood Islands, Prince Edward Island, while the Bay Ferries operates a year-round service between Yarmouth, Nova Scotia and Portland, Maine. Ferry travel is a scenic and leisurely way to see the coastline and enjoy the views.

Guided Tours
If you prefer a more structured and guided approach to exploring Nova Scotia, there are a variety of guided tours available. These tours range from walking tours of historic Halifax to whale-watching expeditions along the Bay of Fundy. Some tour operators even offer customized itineraries based on your interests and preferences.

Accessibility
Nova Scotia is committed to making its transportation options accessible to all visitors, regardless of mobility limitations. Halifax Transit

offers a variety of accessible services, including low-floor buses with wheelchair ramps, priority seating for passengers with disabilities, and specialized transportation services for those who require them. Many car rental companies also offer accessible vehicles, such as vans with wheelchair lifts.

In summary, getting around Nova Scotia is easy and convenient, with a variety of transportation options available to suit every budget and preference. Whether you prefer the freedom of a car rental or the convenience of public transportation, there are plenty of ways to explore the province and discover its hidden gems.

Where to stay in Nova Scotia

When it comes to finding accommodations in Nova Scotia, travelers have plenty of options to choose from. Here are some of the most popular types of lodging in the province:

Hotels and Motels:
Nova Scotia has a variety of hotels and motels ranging from luxury resorts to budget-friendly options. Many hotels and motels are located in popular tourist destinations like Halifax, Cape Breton Island, and the South Shore. Visitors can find comfortable accommodations with a range of

amenities, including swimming pools, restaurants, and fitness centers.

Bed and Breakfasts:
Bed and breakfasts are a popular option for visitors who want to experience the local culture and hospitality. These small inns offer personalized service, home-cooked meals, and a cozy atmosphere. They are often located in historic homes or charming cottages and can be found in rural areas as well as urban centers.

Camping and RV Parks:
Nova Scotia is home to many beautiful camping and RV parks, offering visitors the chance to get closer to nature. These parks range from wilderness camping to full-service RV sites, with amenities such as showers, laundry facilities, and playgrounds. Some popular campgrounds in Nova Scotia include Cape Breton Highlands National Park and Kejimkujik National Park.

Hostels and Guesthouses:
For budget-conscious travelers, hostels and guesthouses offer affordable lodging with basic amenities. These types of accommodations are often located in urban areas and offer shared dormitory-style rooms, as well as private rooms. Hostels and guesthouses can be a great way to meet other travelers and explore the local area.

No matter what type of lodging you choose, it's important to book in advance, especially during peak travel seasons. Additionally, it's always a good idea to read reviews and research the location and amenities to ensure you find the best possible accommodations for your budget and travel needs.

Travel tips for Nova Scotia

Best Time to Visit

- The best time to visit Nova Scotia is from May to October when the weather is mild and most tourist attractions are open.
- However, peak season is July and August, so expect higher prices and bigger crowds.

What to Pack for Your Trip

- Pack for the weather: Nova Scotia has a temperate climate with cool summers and cold winters, so bring layers and a waterproof jacket.
- Bring comfortable walking shoes for exploring cities and hiking trails.
- Bring insect repellent for outdoor activities, especially in summer.
- Don't forget to pack a swimsuit for beaches and lakes.

Language and Communication

- English is the primary language spoken in Nova Scotia, but some locals speak French in Acadian communities.
- Learn some common Canadian phrases, such as "eh?" or "sorry" as they are often used in conversations.

Currency and Tipping

- The currency in Nova Scotia is Canadian dollars (CAD).
- Tipping is common in restaurants and for services such as haircuts and taxis. A standard tip is around 15-20% of the total cost.

Customs and Etiquette

- Nova Scotians are generally friendly and polite, so don't be surprised if someone strikes up a conversation with you.
- It's customary to hold doors open for others and to say "thank you" when someone does something for you.
- Smoking is not allowed in public places, including restaurants and bars.

Additional Tips

- Buy a Nova Scotia Explorer Pass for discounted access to multiple attractions.
- Always check the weather forecast before heading out, as conditions can change quickly.
- Bring a travel adapter if you plan to use electronic devices, as the electrical outlets in Canada are different from those in some other countries.

By following these travel tips, you can ensure a smooth and enjoyable trip to Nova Scotia.

Nova Scotia Travel Itineraries

Nova Scotia offers a diverse range of attractions and experiences, from the bustling city of Halifax to the rugged beauty of Cape Breton Island. Here are three sample itineraries to help you plan your trip:

3-day itinerary: highlights of Halifax and the South Shore

- Day 1: Explore Halifax's historic sites, museums, and galleries, including the Citadel, the Maritime Museum of the Atlantic, and the Art Gallery of Nova Scotia. In the evening, head to the Halifax Waterfront Boardwalk for seafood and live music.

- Day 2: Take a scenic drive down the South Shore, stopping to see Peggy's Cove, Mahone Bay, and Lunenburg, a UNESCO World Heritage Site. In the evening, enjoy a seafood dinner in Chester.
- Day 3: Spend the day hiking or kayaking in Kejimkujik National Park, then head back to Halifax for your departure.

This itinerary is ideal for those who want to experience the best of Halifax, as well as some of the surrounding areas. The itinerary includes a mix of urban sightseeing, coastal drives, and outdoor activities. In Halifax, you can explore the city's history at the Citadel, which is a National Historic Site, or visit one of the many museums or galleries. The Maritime Museum of the Atlantic is a great option for those interested in the province's seafaring history, while the Art Gallery of Nova Scotia showcases the province's vibrant arts scene.

The South Shore of Nova Scotia is known for its scenic beauty and charming coastal towns. Peggy's Cove is one of the most photographed lighthouses in the world, while Lunenburg is a UNESCO World Heritage Site that offers a glimpse into the province's seafaring past. Mahone Bay is a picturesque village with colourful houses and great cafes and restaurants.

7-day itinerary: exploring Cape Breton Island and the Northumberland Shore

- Day 1-2: Drive from Halifax to the Northumberland Shore, stopping to see the tidal bore in Truro and the Joggins Fossil Cliffs. Spend the night in Pictou.
- Day 3-4: Take the ferry to Prince Edward Island for a day trip, then head back to the mainland and drive to Cape Breton Island. Spend the next two days exploring the Cabot Trail, stopping to hike, whale watch, and enjoy the stunning scenery.
- Day 5-6: Drive to Baddeck, the gateway to Cape Breton Highlands National Park. Spend the next two days hiking, fishing, and exploring the charming town of Baddeck.
- Day 7: Return to Halifax for your departure.

This itinerary is perfect for those who want to experience the rugged beauty of Cape Breton Island, as well as the quaint towns and villages of the Northumberland Shore. The itinerary includes some of the province's most iconic attractions, such as the Cabot Trail and Cape Breton Highlands National Park, as well as some off-the-beaten-path destinations, such as Pictou and the Joggins Fossil Cliffs.

Cape Breton Island is a world-famous destination for its natural beauty and outdoor activities. The

Cabot Trail is a scenic drive that offers breathtaking views of the ocean and the mountains, while Cape Breton Highlands National Park is a wilderness paradise with plenty of hiking trails, fishing spots, and wildlife sightings.

The Northumberland Shore of Nova Scotia is known for its historic sites and charming villages. Pictou is the birthplace of New Scotland, and the Hector Heritage Quay museum is a must-visit attraction for those interested in the province's Scottish heritage. The Joggins Fossil Cliffs are a UNESCO World Heritage Site and offer a glimpse into the prehistoric past of the province.

10-day itinerary: a comprehensive tour of Nova Scotia

- Day 1-2: Spend two days exploring Halifax and the surrounding area, including Peggy's Cove and Lunenburg.
- Day 3-4: Drive down the South Shore, stopping to see the Annapolis Valley, Kejimkujik National Park, and Yarmouth. Spend the night in Yarmouth.
- Day 5-6: Take the ferry to Maine, USA for a day trip, then head back to Nova Scotia and drive to Cape Breton Island. Spend two days exploring the Cabot Trail and Cape Breton Highlands National Park.

- Day 7-8: Drive to the Northumberland Shore and spend the next two days exploring the Pictou area and the Joggins Fossil Cliffs.
- Day 9-10: Return to Halifax and spend your final two days visiting the city's museums, galleries, and cultural sites. On your final evening, head to the Halifax Waterfront Boardwalk for a farewell dinner.

This itinerary is perfect for those who want to experience the best of Nova Scotia in one trip. It includes a mix of urban sightseeing, coastal drives, outdoor activities, and cultural experiences. The itinerary covers some of the most iconic destinations in the province, such as Halifax, Peggy's Cove, and the Cabot Trail, as well as some off-the-beaten-path attractions, such as Yarmouth and the Annapolis Valley.

The Annapolis Valley is known for its vineyards and orchards, and it's a great destination for foodies. The Valley is also home to several historic sites, such as the Grand-Pré National Historic Site, which is a UNESCO World Heritage Site.

Yarmouth is a coastal town with a rich seafaring history, and it's a great destination for those interested in the province's maritime heritage. The Yarmouth County Museum and Archives is a must-visit attraction for those interested in the history of the town and the surrounding area.

Remember, these itineraries are just suggestions – feel free to customize them to fit your interests and schedule. With so much to see and do in Nova Scotia, you're sure to have an unforgettable trip!

Chapter 3: Halifax and Surrounding Areas

In this chapter, we'll explore the top things to see and do in Halifax and the surrounding areas, as well as some recommended day trips and the best places to eat in the city. Whether you're a history buff, a foodie, or an outdoor enthusiast, Halifax has something for everyone.

Overview of Halifax

Halifax, the capital city of Nova Scotia, is a bustling and historic port town with a rich maritime heritage. Founded in 1749, it has played an important role in Canadian history, from its early days as a British colonial outpost to its crucial role in World War II.

Today, Halifax is a vibrant and cosmopolitan city with a thriving arts and culture scene, award-winning restaurants, and plenty of outdoor recreational opportunities. Visitors to Halifax can explore its historic landmarks, wander its charming neighborhoods, or take day trips to nearby attractions.

Why Visit Halifax?

There are many reasons to visit Halifax. Here are just a few:

- History: Halifax has a rich history that spans over 250 years. From its early days as a British colonial outpost to its role in the Halifax Explosion of 1917, there is no shortage of fascinating stories to discover in this city.
- Culture: Halifax has a vibrant arts and culture scene, with numerous galleries, museums, theaters, and festivals. Visitors can take in a show at the Neptune Theatre, explore the Halifax Public Gardens, or attend the Halifax International Busker Festival.
- Cuisine: Halifax is known for its fresh seafood, but it also has a diverse food scene that includes everything from Italian to Indian cuisine. Visitors can enjoy a seafood feast at The Five Fishermen, grab a coffee and pastry at Two If By Sea, or sample some of the city's best pub fare at Durty Nelly's.
- Outdoor activities: With its proximity to the Atlantic Ocean, Halifax offers a wide range of outdoor activities, including hiking, kayaking, and whale watching. Visitors can explore the nearby Peggy's Cove, take a stroll along the Halifax Waterfront Boardwalk, or head out for a day trip to Kejimkujik National Park.

Things to see and do in Halifax

Historic Halifax Citadel National Historic Site

The Halifax Citadel is a fortification that dates back to the 18th century, and it played a significant role in the defense of Halifax and the British Empire. It is now a National Historic Site of Canada, and a popular attraction for visitors to Halifax.

History and significance of the Halifax Citadel

The Halifax Citadel was built in 1749, shortly after the founding of Halifax, to protect the city from potential attacks by the French and other foreign powers. Over the years, the Citadel underwent several transformations and expansions, including the addition of underground tunnels, ramparts, and defensive structures.

The Citadel was also used as a military training facility, and during World War I and World War II, it served as the headquarters for the Canadian Army in the Atlantic region. Today, the Halifax Citadel is a symbol of Halifax's military history, and an important reminder of the role that the city played in shaping the nation's identity.

Guided tours and exhibits

Visitors to the Halifax Citadel can take a guided tour of the fortress, led by knowledgeable interpreters dressed in historic military uniforms. The tour covers the Citadel's history, its role in defending Halifax and the British Empire, and the daily life of soldiers stationed there.

The Citadel also features several exhibits that showcase the history and culture of Halifax and its people. These include the Army Museum, which displays a collection of military artifacts and memorabilia, and the Halifax Army Barracks, which is a restored 19th-century military barracks that shows what life was like for soldiers stationed at the Citadel.

Changing of the guard ceremony

One of the highlights of a visit to the Halifax Citadel is the changing of the guard ceremony, which takes place every day during the summer months. The ceremony is a colorful display of military pageantry, and features soldiers dressed in full regalia, marching in formation, and performing intricate drills and maneuvers.

Spectacular views of Halifax Harbour

The Halifax Citadel is situated on a hill overlooking Halifax Harbour, and it offers stunning views of the city and the waterfront. Visitors can climb to the top of the Citadel's ramparts and enjoy panoramic views of the harbor, the city skyline, and the surrounding countryside.

Overall, a visit to the Historic Halifax Citadel National Historic Site is a must for anyone interested in Halifax's military history, or for those who simply want to enjoy spectacular views of the city and learn more about its past.

Maritime Museum of the Atlantic

The Maritime Museum of the Atlantic is a popular attraction in Halifax, offering visitors a fascinating look at the city's maritime history. Located on the waterfront, the museum boasts a collection of over 30,000 artifacts and exhibits that showcase the role of the sea in shaping Nova Scotia's past, present, and future.

One of the highlights of the museum is its extensive collection of artifacts and memorabilia from the sinking of the Titanic, which is an important part of Halifax's history. The museum's Titanic exhibit features items such as personal belongings of the passengers and crew, as well as a replica of one of the ship's lifeboats. Visitors can learn about the rescue efforts and the aftermath of the disaster, as well as the role that Halifax played in recovering the bodies of those who perished.

In addition to the Titanic exhibit, the Maritime Museum of the Atlantic has several other permanent exhibits, including displays on Nova Scotia's shipbuilding industry, the Halifax Explosion, and the Royal Canadian Navy. There are also interactive exhibits that allow visitors to experience what life was like on board a ship, such as a steamship engine and a fishing trawler.

The museum also offers a variety of programs and events throughout the year, including guided tours, workshops, and special exhibitions. Visitors can take a harbor tour on a historic wooden boat or rent a kayak to explore the waterfront on their own. The museum also hosts the annual Halifax International Boat Show, which is the largest boat show in Eastern Canada.

Overall, the Maritime Museum of the Atlantic is a must-visit attraction for anyone interested in the history of Halifax and the sea. With its diverse collection of artifacts and interactive exhibits, the museum provides a unique and engaging experience that is sure to fascinate visitors of all ages.

Halifax Public Gardens

The Halifax Public Gardens is a Victorian-era garden located in the heart of downtown Halifax. It covers an area of 16 acres and is one of the finest examples of a Victorian garden in North America. The gardens were opened in 1867, making them one of the oldest public gardens in Canada.

The gardens are a peaceful oasis in the midst of the bustling city, featuring winding pathways, serene ponds, and seasonal flower displays. Visitors can enjoy the tranquil atmosphere and admire the colorful and fragrant blooms, including tulips, daffodils, and roses. The garden's Victorian bandstand and fountain add to its charm, and the ornate wrought-iron gates provide a grand entrance to the park.

The Halifax Public Gardens are also home to several unique sculptures, including a statue of Winston Churchill, a sundial, and a statue of Queen Victoria. The gardens are a popular spot for picnics, photography, and relaxation, and are a favorite among locals and tourists alike.

Throughout the year, the Halifax Public Gardens host several events and activities, including concerts, picnics, and guided tours. In the summer months, visitors can attend the Sunday concerts at the bandstand, featuring live music from local musicians. The gardens are also a popular spot for wedding and engagement photos, and the city provides permits for professional photography sessions.

Admission to the Halifax Public Gardens is free, and the gardens are open daily from dawn until dusk. The gardens are accessible by foot, bike, or public transit, and there are several nearby parking lots for those arriving by car. Visitors should allow at least an hour to explore the gardens and take in the sights and smells of this beautiful and historic park.

Halifax Waterfront Boardwalk

The Halifax Waterfront Boardwalk is a picturesque walkway along Halifax's bustling waterfront that stretches for approximately 4 kilometers (2.5 miles). It's a popular spot for both tourists and locals alike, offering stunning views of Halifax Harbour, historical landmarks, and lively entertainment venues.

Here are some of the highlights of the Halifax Waterfront Boardwalk:

Historical Ships: The boardwalk is home to several historic ships, including the CSS Acadia, which served as a hydrographic survey vessel for over 50 years, and HMCS Sackville, Canada's oldest naval vessel still afloat. Visitors can explore these ships and learn about their history and significance.

Shops and Restaurants: The Halifax Waterfront Boardwalk is lined with a variety of shops, restaurants, and entertainment venues. There are numerous cafes and restaurants where visitors can sample local cuisine and fresh seafood while taking in the stunning views of the harbour. There are also souvenir shops where visitors can purchase locally made products and gifts.

Events and Festivals: The boardwalk is a hub of activity throughout the year, with a variety of events and festivals taking place. During the summer months, there are live music performances, buskers, and street performers. The boardwalk is also home to several large-scale events, such as the Halifax Busker Festival and the Halifax Jazz Festival.

Historical Landmarks: The Halifax Waterfront Boardwalk is home to several historical landmarks, including the Old Town Clock, a prominent landmark that has been keeping time in Halifax since 1803. The boardwalk also offers stunning views of George's Island and McNabs Island, which served as important fortifications during Halifax's colonial period.

Parks and Green Spaces: The Halifax Waterfront Boardwalk offers several parks and green spaces where visitors can relax and enjoy the scenery. These include the Georges Island National Historic Site and the Halifax Seaport Farmers' Market, which is surrounded by a park with benches and picnic tables.

Overall, the Halifax Waterfront Boardwalk is a must-visit attraction in Halifax, offering a unique blend of history, culture, and entertainment. It's a great place to take a leisurely stroll, grab a bite to eat, and take in the sights and sounds of Halifax's vibrant waterfront.

Art Gallery of Nova Scotia

The Art Gallery of Nova Scotia is located in downtown Halifax and is the premier art museum in the province. It is home to over 18,000 works of art, ranging from historic to contemporary pieces, with a particular focus on local and regional artists. The museum is housed in a modern building and features spacious galleries, an auditorium, an art research library, and classrooms for educational programs and workshops.

One of the Art Gallery of Nova Scotia's most popular exhibits is the permanent collection of folk art, which includes works by well-known Nova Scotia artists such as Maud Lewis and Joe Norris. Other highlights include the Alex Colville collection, which features works by one of Canada's most iconic artists, and the contemporary art collection, which showcases works by artists from Nova Scotia and beyond.

The museum also hosts a range of temporary exhibitions throughout the year, which cover a variety of themes and artistic styles. These exhibits may include painting, sculpture, photography, video installations, and performance art.

In addition to its exhibitions, the Art Gallery of Nova Scotia offers a variety of educational programs and workshops for visitors of all ages. These programs include guided tours, art classes, lectures, and workshops on a range of topics, from drawing and painting to digital media and photography.

The Art Gallery of Nova Scotia is open year-round and admission is free on Thursday evenings. Visitors can also purchase memberships to the museum, which include unlimited admission, discounts on programs and events, and special member-only events.

Overall, the Art Gallery of Nova Scotia is a must-visit destination for art lovers and those interested in exploring the rich cultural heritage of Nova Scotia.

Halifax Central Library

The Halifax Central Library is a modern, award-winning architectural gem located in the heart of downtown Halifax. Opened in 2014, the library has quickly become a popular destination for locals and tourists alike, offering a range of services and activities for all ages.

The library features five floors of books, media, and technology, as well as a rooftop terrace with stunning views of the city. Here are some of the highlights of what visitors can expect when visiting the Halifax Central Library:

- A vast collection of books, music, and movies: The library's collection boasts over 640,000 items, including books, music, movies, and more. Visitors can borrow materials for free with a library card, which can be obtained at the library's welcome desk.

- State-of-the-art technology: The library offers a range of technological resources, including computer workstations, printing and scanning services, and free Wi-Fi throughout the building. There are also meeting rooms available for public use.

- Public events and programs: The library hosts a wide variety of events and programs throughout the year, including author readings, workshops, and educational programs for children and adults. Many of these events are free and open to the public.

- Art installations and exhibits: The library features a range of permanent and rotating art installations and exhibits, including works by local and international artists.

- Halifax Living Room: The Halifax Living Room is a cozy reading space on the library's main floor. Visitors can relax on comfortable couches and chairs while reading or chatting with friends.

- Maker Space: The library's Maker Space is a creative hub that offers tools and resources for visitors to explore their creativity and learn new skills. The space includes 3D printers, a laser cutter, and a vinyl cutter, as well as workshops and programs on topics such as coding, graphic design, and music production.

The Halifax Central Library is a must-see destination for visitors to Halifax, offering a unique blend of modern technology and traditional library services. Visitors can immerse themselves in the city's vibrant culture and learn about its history and community through the library's extensive collection and engaging programs.

Pier 21 National Historic Site

Pier 21 is located on the Halifax waterfront and was once the main immigration gateway to Canada, welcoming over a million immigrants, refugees, and war brides between 1928 and 1971. Today, it is Canada's national immigration museum and a significant part of Halifax's cultural heritage.

The museum offers a range of exhibits and activities that explore the stories of immigrants who have come to Canada, and the role of immigration in shaping Canadian identity. Visitors can explore the stories of people from different backgrounds and cultures, including those who came to Canada to escape war, persecution, and economic hardship.

The exhibits at Pier 21 are interactive and engaging, with artifacts, personal stories, and multimedia presentations. The museum also offers a range of educational programs and resources for students and teachers, including guided tours, workshops, and online learning tools.

One of the highlights of a visit to Pier 21 is the opportunity to trace your own family history. The museum has a Genealogy Centre that houses a wealth of records and resources to help visitors discover their family roots. The centre offers one-on-one consultations with staff genealogists, access to databases and archives, and workshops on genealogical research.

In addition to the exhibits and genealogy centre, Pier 21 offers a range of other activities and events. Visitors can attend lectures, book launches, and film screenings, or participate in a cultural event or festival. The museum also hosts special exhibitions throughout the year, which showcase the work of Canadian artists and explore themes related to immigration, diversity, and inclusion.

Overall, Pier 21 National Historic Site is a must-visit attraction in Halifax for anyone interested in Canadian history, immigration, and cultural diversity. It offers a unique and moving perspective on the experiences of people who have come to Canada, and the role of immigration in shaping the country's past, present, and future.

Canadian Museum of Immigration

The Canadian Museum of Immigration is located in the historic Pier 21 building on the Halifax waterfront, which served as a hub of immigration to Canada from 1928 to 1971. Today, the museum is dedicated to preserving the stories and experiences of the millions of people who have come to Canada seeking a better life.

Exhibits:

The museum's exhibits provide a comprehensive look at the history of Canadian immigration, highlighting the many challenges and opportunities that newcomers have faced throughout the years. The exhibits feature interactive displays, personal stories, and artifacts, offering a unique and engaging experience for visitors of all ages.

Some of the key exhibits include:

The Canadian Immigration Story: This exhibit provides an overview of Canadian immigration history, from the arrival of the First Nations to the present day. It highlights the various waves of immigration that have shaped Canada's cultural landscape, including the experiences of Indigenous peoples, African Canadians, and newcomers from all over the world.

Canada by Boat: This exhibit tells the story of the ocean liners that brought millions of immigrants to Canada in the early 20th century. It features artifacts and memorabilia from the ships, as well as personal stories of the passengers who made the journey.

Leaving Home: This exhibit explores the many reasons why people choose to leave their homes and come to Canada, including economic hardship, war, and political persecution. It features stories and artifacts from immigrants of all backgrounds, from Chinese railway workers to Syrian refugees.

Destination Canada: This exhibit showcases the many ways in which immigrants have contributed to Canadian society, including in the arts, sciences, and sports. It also provides information on the immigration process today, highlighting the various programs and services available to newcomers.

Special Events:

The museum also hosts a range of special events throughout the year, including workshops, lectures, and cultural celebrations. These events offer visitors a chance to learn more about specific aspects of Canadian immigration history and to connect with other members of the community.

Research Services:

For visitors interested in tracing their family history, the museum offers a range of research services, including access to immigration records, genealogy workshops, and one-on-one consultations with research experts.

Overall, the Canadian Museum of Immigration is an essential stop for anyone interested in the history and culture of Canada. Through its exhibits, events, and research services, it provides a window into the many experiences and contributions of Canada's diverse immigrant communities.

Halifax Seaport Farmers' Market

The Halifax Seaport Farmers' Market is a must-visit destination for anyone looking to experience the authentic flavors of Nova Scotia. Founded in 1750, it is the oldest continuously operating farmers' market in Canada, and has been housed in its current location on the Halifax waterfront since 2010.

The market is home to over 250 vendors, offering everything from fresh produce, seafood, meat, and dairy products to artisanal crafts, clothing, jewelry, and souvenirs. Visitors can browse the stalls and sample the goods, all while taking in the lively atmosphere of the market.

In addition to the vendors, the market also features several restaurants and food stands, offering a wide variety of local cuisine. Whether you're in the mood for seafood chowder, lobster rolls, smoked salmon, or freshly baked bread, there is something for everyone at the Halifax Seaport Farmers' Market.

The market is also a hub of Halifax's cultural scene, hosting live music, art exhibitions, and other special events throughout the year. Visitors can learn about Nova Scotia's rich cultural heritage through interactive exhibits and displays, or attend cooking demonstrations and classes to learn how to prepare local dishes at home.

The Halifax Seaport Farmers' Market is open year-round, with hours varying depending on the season. During the summer months, the market is especially busy, with crowds of locals and tourists flocking to the waterfront to enjoy the food, music, and scenery.

Overall, the Halifax Seaport Farmers' Market is a must-see destination for anyone interested in experiencing the authentic flavors and culture of Nova Scotia.

St. Mary's Basilica

St. Mary's Basilica is one of the most impressive churches in Halifax, located in the city's downtown area. Built in 1820, the church features stunning Gothic Revival architecture and beautiful stained glass windows. It is the oldest Roman Catholic church in Halifax and an important landmark for the city.

Visitors to St. Mary's Basilica can take a guided tour of the church, which includes an overview of its history, architecture, and notable features. The tour highlights the church's intricate woodwork, impressive stone carvings, and intricate stained glass windows, which were crafted in Europe and shipped to Halifax.

St. Mary's Basilica is also known for its impressive choir, which performs a series of concerts throughout the year. These concerts showcase the church's exceptional acoustics and feature a range of musical styles, from classical to contemporary.

In addition to its regular services and events, St. Mary's Basilica also hosts special events throughout the year, including holiday masses, community events, and cultural celebrations. Visitors are encouraged to check the church's schedule in advance to see if any special events or performances are taking place during their visit.

For those interested in the history and architecture of St. Mary's Basilica, the church offers a wealth of resources, including books, videos, and educational materials. Visitors can also purchase souvenirs and gifts at the church's gift shop, which features a range of religious items and local products.

Overall, St. Mary's Basilica is a must-visit attraction for anyone interested in the history, architecture, and culture of Halifax. It offers a unique and inspiring experience that is sure to leave a lasting impression on visitors.

Day trips from Halifax

Peggy's Cove

Located about 43 kilometers (27 miles) southwest of Halifax, Peggy's Cove is a charming fishing village and popular day trip destination from Halifax. The village is known for its iconic lighthouse, which was built in 1915 and stands on top of a large granite rock overlooking the ocean. Peggy's Cove is also known for its stunning rocky coastline, which makes it a popular spot for photography.

Visitors to Peggy's Cove can explore the village's historic buildings, browse local art galleries and souvenir shops, and enjoy fresh seafood at one of the village's many restaurants. There are several hiking trails in the area, including the easy Peggy's Cove Coastal Trail, which takes visitors along the rocky coastline and offers stunning views of the Atlantic Ocean.

While the lighthouse is undoubtedly the main attraction in Peggy's Cove, visitors should exercise caution when exploring the rocks around it, as they can be slippery and dangerous, especially during high tide. The area is also subject to unpredictable weather conditions, so it's important to dress appropriately and be prepared for changes in temperature, wind, and precipitation.

Overall, Peggy's Cove is a must-see destination for anyone visiting Nova Scotia. Its stunning natural beauty and rich history make it a popular spot for tourists and locals alike.

Lunenburg

Lunenburg is a charming and historic town located about 90 minutes from Halifax. It was founded in 1753 and has been designated a UNESCO World Heritage Site for its well-preserved 18th-century architecture, including colorful wooden houses, churches, and public buildings.

One of the town's most notable attractions is the Fisheries Museum of the Atlantic, which tells the story of the town's maritime history and the fishing industry that has sustained it for centuries. The museum features exhibits on boatbuilding, fishing techniques, and the town's role in the famous Bluenose schooner races.

Visitors to Lunenburg can also tour the historic Bluenose II schooner, which is a replica of the original Bluenose that was built in Lunenburg in 1921. The ship is a symbol of Nova Scotia's seafaring heritage and is one of Canada's most famous sailing vessels.

Another popular attraction in Lunenburg is the town's colorful waterfront, which is home to a variety of shops, cafes, and restaurants. Visitors can browse local art galleries, sample fresh seafood, or take a stroll along the boardwalk.

In addition to its historic and cultural attractions, Lunenburg is also known for its lively arts scene. The town is home to several theaters and music venues, including the Lunenburg Opera House and the Lunenburg Folk Harbour Society.

Overall, Lunenburg is a charming and picturesque town that offers visitors a glimpse into Nova Scotia's rich maritime history and cultural heritage. Whether you're interested in history, art, or simply relaxing by the water, Lunenburg is definitely worth a visit.

Mahone Bay

Mahone Bay is a charming coastal town located about an hour's drive from Halifax. The town is known for its beautiful harbor, which is dotted with dozens of small islands, and for its three iconic churches, which are a popular spot for photography.

Visitors to Mahone Bay can explore the town's quaint shops and cafes, many of which are housed in historic buildings that date back to the town's founding in the 18th century. Artisans and craftspeople have long been drawn to the town, and visitors can browse local galleries showcasing everything from pottery and jewelry to paintings and textiles.

One of the best ways to experience Mahone Bay is to take a boat tour of the harbor. Several local companies offer tours that take visitors to explore the many islands in the bay and to get a closer look at the town's picturesque waterfront.

For those who prefer to stay on land, there are plenty of hiking trails and beaches in and around Mahone Bay. The nearby Graves Island Provincial Park is a popular spot for camping, swimming, and hiking, and is known for its beautiful sandy beach.

Mahone Bay is also known for its many festivals and events throughout the year. In the summer, the town hosts a weekly farmers' market, as well as an annual regatta that draws crowds from all over Nova Scotia. The town is also home to several annual craft and artisan fairs, as well as a popular Christmas market that showcases the town's festive holiday spirit.

Annapolis Royal

Annapolis Royal is a charming historic town located about 2 hours from Halifax, known for its rich colonial past and numerous cultural attractions. Here are some of the things to see and do in Annapolis Royal:

Historic Gardens: The Historic Gardens are a popular destination in Annapolis Royal, featuring over 17 acres of beautiful gardens and historic buildings. Visitors can stroll through themed gardens including a rose garden, an herb garden, and a Victorian garden, and explore the garden's many historic buildings, including a Victorian-era summer house and a 17th-century Acadian dyke house.

Fort Anne National Historic Site: Located on the banks of the Annapolis River, the Fort Anne National Historic Site is a well-preserved 17th-century fort that played a key role in the early colonial history of Nova Scotia. Visitors can explore the fort's many historic buildings and exhibits, including a restored barracks and a museum dedicated to the history of the fort and the surrounding area.

Annapolis Royal Historic District: The Annapolis Royal Historic District is a designated National Historic Site of Canada, featuring over 135 historic buildings and sites, including the oldest wooden house in Canada. Visitors can take a self-guided walking tour of the district, which includes several historic churches, homes, and businesses.

Art galleries and boutiques: Annapolis Royal is known for its thriving arts and culture scene, with numerous art galleries, craft shops, and boutiques showcasing the work of local artists and artisans. Visitors can browse for unique souvenirs, jewelry, and other handmade goods, or attend one of the many art exhibitions and events held throughout the year.

Dining: Annapolis Royal has several popular restaurants serving up locally-sourced cuisine, including seafood, farm-to-table dishes, and traditional Acadian cuisine. Visitors can enjoy a meal at one of the town's many restaurants, cafes, or bakeries, or sample some of the town's delicious ice cream or fudge.

Overall, Annapolis Royal is a charming town with a rich history and numerous cultural attractions, making it a must-visit destination for anyone traveling to Nova Scotia.

Wolfville

Located in the heart of Nova Scotia's wine country, Wolfville is a charming university town known for its thriving arts and culture scene. The town is surrounded by lush green farmland, rolling hills, and vineyards, making it a great destination for nature lovers and wine enthusiasts alike.

One of the top attractions in Wolfville is the Grand-Pré National Historic Site, which commemorates the Acadian people and their expulsion from Nova Scotia in the 18th century. The site features a visitor center, a reconstructed Acadian home, and a memorial church, all of which provide a fascinating glimpse into the region's history.

Another popular activity in Wolfville is wine touring, as the town is surrounded by numerous wineries and vineyards. Visitors can explore the Gaspereau Valley Wine Country, which is home to several award-winning wineries, including Luckett Vineyards, Lightfoot & Wolfville, and Benjamin Bridge. Wine lovers can take a guided tour of the wineries and vineyards, sample the wines, and enjoy the beautiful scenery.

For nature lovers, there are several hiking trails and parks in and around Wolfville. One of the most popular trails is the Cape Split trail, which offers stunning views of the Bay of Fundy and the surrounding coastline. The trail is about a 1.5-hour hike each way and is suitable for intermediate hikers.

The town of Wolfville also has a thriving arts and culture scene, with several galleries, museums, and theaters. The Acadia University Art Gallery is a must-visit for art lovers, as it showcases contemporary and historical artwork from local and international artists. The Al Whittle Theatre is a popular venue for live music, theater, and film screenings.

Finally, Wolfville has several restaurants and cafes serving up delicious farm-to-table cuisine. The town's culinary scene is inspired by the region's abundant local produce, seafood, and wine. Some of the top restaurants in Wolfville include the Le Caveau Restaurant, the Tempest Restaurant, and the Noodle Guy.

Overall, Wolfville offers a perfect combination of natural beauty, history, wine, and culture, making it a must-visit day trip destination from Halifax.

Grand-Pré National Historic Site

Located in the Annapolis Valley, about 1.5 hours from Halifax, the Grand-Pré National Historic Site is a UNESCO World Heritage Site that commemorates the Acadian people and their expulsion from Nova Scotia in the 18th century. The site includes a visitor center, a reconstructed Acadian home, and a memorial church. Visitors can take a guided tour of the site or explore on their own.

The visitor center features exhibits that tell the story of the Acadian people and their rich cultural heritage. Visitors can learn about the early French settlement of Nova Scotia and the struggle for control of the territory between the French and British. The exhibits also explore the tragic story of the Acadian deportation, which saw thousands of

Acadians forcibly removed from their homes and sent to other British colonies or back to France.

The reconstructed Acadian home gives visitors a glimpse into the daily life of the Acadian people. The home is furnished with period-appropriate furniture and artifacts, and costumed interpreters provide demonstrations of traditional Acadian activities such as cooking and spinning wool.

The memorial church is a striking modern structure that was built in 1922 to honor the Acadian people. The church features a series of stained-glass windows that tell the story of the Acadian expulsion, as well as a bronze statue of Evangeline, a character from Longfellow's famous poem who represents the Acadian people.

In addition to the visitor center, home, and church, the Grand-Pré National Historic Site also features beautiful grounds that visitors can explore. The site is surrounded by lush gardens and orchards, and visitors can take a peaceful stroll along the walking trails that wind through the property.

Overall, the Grand-Pré National Historic Site is a must-visit destination for anyone interested in Nova Scotia's rich history and cultural heritage. The site offers a fascinating look into the lives of the Acadian people and their tragic expulsion from the province, and provides a moving tribute to their enduring legacy.

Kejimkujik National Park

Kejimkujik National Park is a 404 square kilometer park located in the southwestern part of Nova Scotia. The park is home to an impressive array of wildlife, including moose, black bears, beavers, and a variety of bird species. Visitors to the park can participate in a wide range of outdoor activities, including hiking, camping, paddling, and fishing.

Hiking is a popular activity in the park, with over 15 trails to choose from. Some of the most popular hikes include the Hemlocks and Hardwoods Trail, which leads through a dense forest of hemlock and hardwood trees, and the Mill Falls Trail, which leads to a picturesque waterfall. The park also offers several longer backpacking trails for those looking for a multi-day adventure.

Paddling is another popular activity in the park, with over 20 lakes and ponds to explore. The park offers canoe, kayak, and stand-up paddleboard rentals, as well as guided paddling tours. Fishing is also allowed in many of the park's lakes and streams, with a variety of fish species available, including trout, bass, and pickerel.

For those looking to camp in the park, there are several campgrounds to choose from. The main campground, Jeremy's Bay, offers over 350 campsites, including both serviced and unserviced sites. The park also offers backcountry camping options for those looking to get off the beaten path.

In addition to outdoor activities, Kejimkujik National Park is also home to several historic sites, including a Mi'kmaw petroglyph site and several ancient burial grounds. The park also offers several interpretive programs and guided hikes, where visitors can learn about the park's natural and cultural history.

Overall, Kejimkujik National Park is a must-visit destination for outdoor enthusiasts visiting Nova Scotia. With its stunning natural beauty, diverse wildlife, and wide range of activities, it's the perfect place to immerse yourself in the great outdoors.

Digby and the Bay of Fundy

Located about 2.5 hours from Halifax, Digby is a charming town that sits on the shores of the Bay of Fundy, which is known for having the highest tides in the world. Visitors to Digby can explore the town's many seafood restaurants, which serve up fresh local catches like Digby scallops, lobster, and haddock.

One popular attraction in the area is the Digby Pines Golf Resort and Spa, which features a world-class golf course and a luxurious spa. Visitors can also take a whale watching tour of the Bay of Fundy, which is home to several species of whales, including humpbacks, fin whales, and minke whales. The area is also popular for birdwatching, with several species of seabirds and shorebirds found in the region.

Another popular activity in the area is hiking the nearby trails, including the UNESCO-designated Biosphere Reserve of the Tobeatic Wilderness Area. The area is also home to several parks and nature reserves, including the Annapolis Basin Look Off Provincial Park and the Delaps Cove Wilderness Trail.

For those interested in history and culture, the nearby town of Annapolis Royal features several historic sites, including Fort Anne National Historic Site, which is the oldest national historic site in Canada. The town also features several museums and galleries showcasing local art and culture.

Overall, a day trip to Digby and the Bay of Fundy is a great way to experience the natural beauty, history, and culture of Nova Scotia's south shore.

Cape Breton Island (overnight trip)

Cape Breton Island is a must-visit destination for anyone exploring Nova Scotia. Located about a four-hour drive from Halifax, it's best to plan an overnight trip to really take in all the island has to offer. The island is known for its stunning natural beauty, which includes rugged coastal cliffs, rolling hills, and lush forests.

One of the main attractions on Cape Breton Island is the Cabot Trail, a scenic drive that winds along the island's coast and through the Cape Breton Highlands National Park. The drive takes about 5-6 hours to complete, but visitors should plan for longer to really take in the stunning scenery and to stop for photos and hikes along the way. There are several lookout points and hiking trails along the Cabot Trail, including the Skyline Trail and the Franey Trail, both of which offer stunning views of the surrounding landscape.

Another popular attraction on Cape Breton Island is the Fortress of Louisbourg National Historic Site, a reconstruction of an 18th-century French fortress that was once one of the busiest seaports in North America. Visitors can explore the reconstructed buildings and interact with costumed interpreters who bring the history of the fortress to life.

In addition to the Cabot Trail and the Fortress of Louisbourg, there are several charming towns and villages to explore on Cape Breton Island. Baddeck, located on the shores of the Bras d'Or Lake, is known for its association with Alexander Graham Bell and features several museums and historic sites dedicated to the inventor. Inverness, located on the island's west coast, is known for its beautiful sandy beach and is a popular spot for surfing. Chéticamp, located on the island's northeast coast, is a vibrant Acadian community and is a great place to experience the local culture.

Visitors to Cape Breton Island can also enjoy a variety of outdoor activities, including hiking, fishing, kayaking, and whale watching. The island is home to several golf courses, including the highly-regarded Cabot Links and Cabot Cliffs, which offer stunning views of the ocean.

Overall, Cape Breton Island is a must-visit destination for anyone exploring Nova Scotia. With its stunning natural beauty, rich history, and vibrant culture, it's no wonder the island is consistently ranked as one of the top tourist destinations in Canada.

Where to eat in Halifax

Seafood Restaurants:
Halifax is known for its fresh seafood, and there are several restaurants in the city that specialize in serving up locally-sourced fish and shellfish. The

Five Fishermen is a popular seafood restaurant located in a historic building on Barrington Street. The menu features a wide variety of seafood dishes, including lobster, scallops, and halibut. The Press Gang is another popular seafood restaurant located in a historic building on Prince Street. The menu features a wide variety of fresh seafood dishes, as well as a selection of cocktails and fine wines. Salty's is a popular seafood restaurant located on the Halifax waterfront. The menu features a wide variety of seafood dishes, including fish and chips, clam chowder, and lobster.

Italian Cuisine:

Halifax also has a thriving Italian restaurant scene, with several restaurants serving up authentic Italian dishes. Il Mercato is a popular Italian restaurant located on Spring Garden Road. The menu features a variety of classic Italian dishes, including homemade pasta, pizza, and antipasti. Ristorante a Mano is another popular Italian restaurant located on Brunswick Street. The menu features a variety of fresh pasta dishes, as well as seafood and meat dishes. La Frasca is a cozy Italian restaurant located on Spring Garden Road. The menu features a variety of homemade pasta dishes, as well as meat and seafood dishes.

Fine Dining:

For those looking for a more upscale dining experience, Halifax has several fine dining restaurants. Edna is a popular restaurant located on Gottingen Street. The menu features a variety of seasonal dishes, as well as a selection of fine wines and cocktails. Cut Steakhouse is a popular steakhouse located on Lower Water Street. The menu features a variety of high-quality steaks, as well as seafood and vegetarian options. The Barrington Steakhouse and Oyster Bar is another popular fine dining restaurant located on Barrington Street. The menu features a variety of steak and seafood dishes, as well as an extensive wine list.

Pub Fare:
Halifax has a thriving pub scene, with several pubs serving up classic pub fare. Durty Nelly's is a popular pub located on Argyle Street. The menu features a variety of classic pub dishes, including fish and chips, shepherd's pie, and bangers and mash. The Old Triangle is another popular pub located on Prince Street. The menu features a variety of pub dishes, as well as live music and entertainment. The Henry House is a popular gastropub located on Barrington Street. The menu features a variety of pub dishes, as well as a selection of craft beers and fine wines.

Coffee Shops and Bakeries:

For those looking for a quick bite or a sweet treat, Halifax has several coffee shops and bakeries. Two If By Sea is a popular coffee shop located on Ochterloney Street in Dartmouth. The menu features a variety of fresh-baked pastries, as well as coffee and tea. The Coastal Café is another popular coffee shop located on Robie Street. The menu features a variety of breakfast and brunch dishes, as well as coffee and tea. Julien's Patisserie is a popular bakery located on Hollis Street. The menu features a variety of fresh-baked pastries, cakes, and macarons.

Farm-to-Table:
Halifax also has a growing farm-to-table restaurant scene, with several restaurants serving up locally-sourced and seasonal ingredients. The Bicycle Thief is a popular farm-to-table restaurant located on Lower Water Street. The menu features a variety of fresh seafood dishes, as well as meat and vegetarian options. Field Guide is another popular farm-to-table restaurant located on Gottingen Street. The menu features a variety of seasonal dishes, as well as a selection of craft cocktails and fine wines. Agricola Street Brasserie is a cozy farm-to-table restaurant located on Agricola Street. The menu features a variety of seasonal dishes, as well as a selection of craft beers and fine wines.

Food Trucks:

Halifax has a growing food truck scene, with several food trucks serving up a variety of cuisine. The Food Wolf is a popular food truck that serves up gourmet sandwiches and poutine. The Gecko Bus is another popular food truck that serves up fresh and healthy Mexican cuisine. The Halifax Donair and Pizza Bus is a popular food truck that serves up classic Halifax donairs and pizza.

In conclusion, Halifax is a foodie's paradise, with a wide variety of restaurants and eateries to suit any taste or budget. Whether you're in the mood for fresh seafood, authentic Italian cuisine, fine dining, pub fare, coffee and pastries, farm-to-table, or food trucks, Halifax has got you covered. Be sure to explore the city's vibrant food scene on your next trip to Nova Scotia!

Chapter 4: South Shore and Annapolis Valley

Overview of the South Shore and Annapolis Valley

The South Shore and Annapolis Valley regions of Nova Scotia are located on the eastern coast of Canada, south of Halifax. The area is known for its scenic beauty, historic towns and villages, and agricultural heritage. The South Shore is home to some of the most picturesque coastal towns in Canada, including Lunenburg, Mahone Bay, and Chester. The Annapolis Valley is famous for its fertile farmland and vineyards, producing some of the best wines in the region.

Lunenburg is a UNESCO World Heritage Site, famous for its brightly painted wooden houses and historic architecture. It was founded in 1753 as a British colonial settlement, and its shipbuilding and fishing industries were instrumental in shaping the region's history. Today, Lunenburg is a popular tourist destination, with many attractions and activities, including museums, art galleries, and boat tours.

Mahone Bay is another charming coastal town on the South Shore, known for its picturesque waterfront, unique shops and galleries, and traditional architecture. The town is home to the famous three churches, St. James Anglican Church, Trinity United Church, and St. John's Evangelical Lutheran Church, which are a popular destination for photographers and artists.

The Annapolis Valley is a fertile valley running parallel to the Bay of Fundy. The valley is home to numerous vineyards, orchards, and farmers' markets, where visitors can taste some of the best local produce, including apples, berries, and grapes. The region is also famous for its historic sites, including the Grand-Pré National Historic Site, which tells the story of the Acadian people who settled in the area in the 17th century.

Overall, the South Shore and Annapolis Valley are two of the most beautiful and historically rich regions in Nova Scotia. With their charming towns, stunning coastlines, and fertile farmland, they offer visitors a unique glimpse into the culture and history of this part of Canada.

Things to see and do in the South Shore and Annapolis Valley

Visit the UNESCO World Heritage Site of Old Town Lunenburg and learn about the town's shipbuilding and fishing history:

Old Town Lunenburg is a well-preserved British colonial town that was designated a UNESCO World Heritage Site in 1995. Visitors can take a walking tour of the town's colorful houses and historic buildings, which date back to the 18th and 19th centuries. The Fisheries Museum of the Atlantic is also located in Lunenburg, and offers a fascinating look at the region's fishing history, including interactive exhibits and displays of fishing gear, boats, and models.

Explore the charming coastal town of Mahone Bay, known for its picturesque waterfront and unique shops and galleries:

Mahone Bay is a small coastal town that is known for its charming waterfront, which is dotted with colorful wooden boats and houses. Visitors can take a stroll along the town's three churches, which are all within a short distance of each other and offer unique architecture and history. Mahone Bay is also home to many unique shops and galleries, offering a chance to browse for handcrafted goods and artwork.

Take a stroll along the beautiful beaches of Queensland, Crescent, and Rissers Provincial Park:

The South Shore is home to many beautiful beaches that offer visitors a chance to relax and enjoy the scenic beauty of the region. Queensland Beach, Crescent Beach, and Rissers Provincial Park are all popular destinations that offer sandy shores, clear waters, and stunning views of the ocean. Rissers Provincial Park also offers camping facilities and hiking trails.

Discover the Annapolis Valley's agricultural heritage by visiting local wineries, orchards, and farmers' markets:

The Annapolis Valley is known for its rich agricultural heritage, and visitors can explore this aspect of the region by visiting local wineries, orchards, and farmers' markets. Wineries such as Luckett Vineyards and Domaine de Grand Pré offer tastings of locally produced wines, while orchards such as Noggins Corner Farm and Masstown Market offer pick-your-own apples and other fruits in season. Farmers' markets such as the Wolfville Farmers' Market offer a chance to sample local produce and artisanal goods.

Take a hike on the Kejimkujik National Park Seaside Trail, which offers stunning views of the Atlantic Ocean and coastal landscape:

The Kejimkujik National Park Seaside Trail is a scenic hiking trail that offers stunning views of the Atlantic Ocean and the rugged coastal landscape of the South Shore. The trail is 8.5 km long and takes hikers through coastal forests, salt marshes, and along rocky shores. Visitors can spot seals, shorebirds, and other wildlife along the trail.

Visit the Grand-Pré National Historic Site and learn about the region's Acadian history and culture:

The Grand-Pré National Historic Site is a UNESCO World Heritage Site that commemorates the history of the Acadian people in Nova Scotia. The site features interpretive exhibits and displays that tell the story of the Acadian people, including their deportation by the British in 1755. Visitors can also take guided tours of the site and visit the Acadian Memorial and the Church of St. Charles.

Day trips from the South Shore and Annapolis Valley

Visit the historic town of Annapolis Royal:
Annapolis Royal is a charming town located on the Annapolis River, about an hour's drive from the South Shore. The town is known for its many museums, gardens, and historic sites. You can start your visit with a stroll through the Historic Gardens, which showcase the region's flora and fauna. Next, visit Fort Anne National Historic Site, a 17th-century fortification that played a key role in the early European colonization of the region. You can also visit the Annapolis Royal Historic District, which features over 135 historic properties, including the oldest wooden house in Canada. Other notable attractions include the Sinclair Inn Museum, the O'Dell House Museum, and the Annapolis Royal Farmers' Market.

Take a ferry to McNabs Island:
McNabs Island is a beautiful natural oasis located in the middle of Halifax Harbour. The island is accessible by ferry from the Eastern Passage, which is about an hour's drive from the South Shore. Once on the island, you can explore its many hiking trails, beaches, and historic fortifications. The island is home to Fort McNab National Historic Site, which was built in the late 19th century to defend Halifax Harbour. The fortifications include a series of gun batteries, underground tunnels, and barracks. You

can also visit the McNabs Island Lighthouse, which dates back to 1869.

Visit the Halifax Citadel National Historic Site:
The Halifax Citadel is a star-shaped fortress located in the heart of downtown Halifax. The site played a key role in the defense of Halifax Harbour during the 19th century. Today, it is a national historic site that offers visitors a glimpse into Halifax's military history and role in the British Empire. You can take a guided tour of the fortifications and learn about the soldiers who lived and worked there. You can also watch the daily firing of the noon gun, which is a tradition that dates back to the 1800s. In addition, the Citadel features a museum, a gift shop, and a café.

Explore Peggy's Cove:
Peggy's Cove is a small fishing village located on the rugged Atlantic coast, about an hour's drive from the South Shore. The village is known for its iconic lighthouse, which sits on top of a massive granite outcropping. Visitors can explore the village's narrow streets and colorful houses, and enjoy fresh seafood at one of the local restaurants. You can also take a guided walking tour of the village and learn about its history and culture. For a more active experience, you can hike along the nearby Peggy's

Cove Coastal Trail, which offers stunning views of the ocean and coastline.

Visit the Ross Farm Museum:
The Ross Farm Museum is a living history museum located in New Ross, about an hour's drive from the South Shore. The museum features a collection of historic buildings and artifacts that showcase the region's agricultural heritage. Visitors can see live farm animals, watch demonstrations of traditional crafts and skills, and learn about the daily life of a 19th-century farming family. The museum also hosts special events and programs throughout the year, including a popular harvest festival in the fall.

Take a whale watching tour:
Nova Scotia's waters are home to a variety of whale species, including humpback, minke, and fin whales. Several whale watching tours depart from the South Shore and Annapolis Valley, offering visitors a chance to see these magnificent creatures up close. Tours typically last several hours and include a knowledgeable guide who can provide insights into the whales' behavior and biology. Some tours also include other wildlife sightings, such as seals, dolphins, and seabirds.

These day trips offer a wide range of experiences for visitors to the South Shore and Annapolis Valley, from exploring historic towns and fortifications to hiking along scenic coastal trails and spotting whales in the wild. No matter what your interests, there is sure to be something to suit your taste in this beautiful and fascinating region of Nova Scotia.

Where to eat in the South Shore and Annapolis Valley

Nova Scotia is known for its fresh seafood, and the South Shore and Annapolis Valley regions have plenty of restaurants that serve up delicious dishes made with locally-sourced ingredients. Some of the most popular seafood restaurants in the area include The Old Fish Factory in Lunenburg and The Trellis Cafe in Hubbards.

In addition to seafood, there are also plenty of restaurants in the region that specialize in farm-to-table cuisine. The Flying Apron Cookery in Summerville is a popular spot for those who want to sample the freshest ingredients from local farms and gardens. The restaurant offers a daily changing menu that features dishes such as Nova Scotia duck breast with maple glaze and homemade gnocchi with roasted garlic cream sauce.

For those who want to experience the flavors of international cuisine, there are several restaurants in the area that offer a diverse range of options. The Noodle Guy in Wolfville is a popular spot for those who crave authentic Asian cuisine, while La Torta Woodfired Pizzeria in Wolfville offers delicious

Neapolitan-style pizzas made with fresh, locally-sourced ingredients.

In addition to restaurants, there are also several wineries and cideries in the region that offer tastings and tours. Luckett Vineyards, located in the Gaspereau Valley, is known for its award-winning wines and stunning views of the Annapolis Valley. Domaine de Grand Pré is another popular winery that offers tastings, tours, and a restaurant that specializes in French cuisine.

Another popular restaurant in the South Shore and Annapolis Valley region is The Press Gang, located in downtown Halifax. This restaurant specializes in seafood, steak, and game dishes, with an emphasis on locally-sourced ingredients. The Press Gang's elegant dining room and extensive wine list make it a great spot for a special occasion or romantic dinner.

For those looking for a more casual dining experience, there are several cafes and bakeries in the area that offer delicious baked goods, sandwiches, and coffee. The Biscuit Eater Cafe and Books in Mahone Bay is a cozy spot that serves up homemade soups, sandwiches, and desserts. The Union Street Cafe in Berwick is another popular spot that offers a range of delicious baked goods, including croissants, scones, and breads.

In addition to traditional dining options, there are also several food trucks and markets in the region that offer a variety of tasty treats. The Halifax Seaport Farmers' Market is a popular destination for foodies, with over 250 vendors selling everything from fresh produce to artisanal cheeses and chocolates. The Food Wolf food truck is another popular spot, known for its creative and delicious street food offerings.

Finally, it's worth mentioning that Nova Scotia is also known for its craft beer scene. The South Shore and Annapolis Valley regions are home to several breweries and taprooms, including Boxing Rock Brewing Company in Shelburne and Sea Level Brewing in Port Williams. These breweries offer tours and tastings, giving visitors a chance to sample some of Nova Scotia's best craft beers.

Overall, the South Shore and Annapolis Valley regions offer a diverse range of dining options that cater to every taste and budget. Whether you're in the mood for fresh seafood, farm-to-table cuisine, or craft beer, you're sure to find something that satisfies your appetite in this beautiful corner of Nova Scotia.

Chapter 5: Cape Breton Island

Overview of Cape Breton Island

Cape Breton Island is a beautiful and diverse island located off the northeastern coast of Nova Scotia, Canada. It is part of the Cape Breton Regional Municipality and has a population of approximately 130,000 people. The island is connected to mainland Nova Scotia by the Canso Causeway and is accessible by car, bus, or ferry.

Geographical and historical background of Cape Breton Island:

Cape Breton Island is home to a diverse range of landscapes, including mountains, forests, lakes, and rugged coastline. The island was originally inhabited by the Mi'kmaq people before being colonized by the French in the early 17th century. It was later ceded to the British in 1763 and became an important center for coal mining, fishing, and shipbuilding.

Climate and weather patterns on the Island:
Cape Breton Island has a maritime climate with cool summers and mild winters. The island experiences a fair amount of precipitation throughout the year, with most of the rainfall occurring in the fall and

winter months. Snowfall is also common during the winter months, particularly in the higher elevations.

Best time to visit Cape Breton Island:

The best time to visit Cape Breton Island depends on your interests and preferences. Summer months (June to August) are the peak tourist season and offer the best weather for outdoor activities such as hiking, camping, and whale watching. Fall (September to November) is a great time to visit if you want to experience the stunning fall foliage and attend cultural events such as the Celtic Colours International Festival. Winter months (December to February) offer a quieter and more peaceful atmosphere, with opportunities for winter sports such as skiing and snowshoeing.

Overall, Cape Breton Island's unique geography, rich history, and diverse culture make it a must-visit destination for travelers to Nova Scotia.

Things to see and do in Cape Breton Island

Cabot Trail:

The Cabot Trail is a scenic drive that loops around the northern part of Cape Breton Island. The 300-

kilometer (185-mile) route offers breathtaking views of the ocean, cliffs, and mountains. Along the way, visitors can stop at lookouts, hiking trails, and small fishing villages. The Cabot Trail is one of the most iconic attractions in Nova Scotia, and it's a must-see for any visitor to Cape Breton Island.

Cape Breton Highlands National Park:

Located along the Cabot Trail, Cape Breton Highlands National Park is a 950-square-kilometer (366-square-mile) park that offers a variety of outdoor activities. The park features hiking trails that range from easy walks to challenging hikes, including the Skyline Trail, which offers panoramic views of the ocean and mountains. The park also has camping sites, picnic areas, and scenic lookouts.

Fortress of Louisbourg National Historic Site:

The Fortress of Louisbourg is a restored 18th-century French fortress that offers visitors a glimpse into life in the colonial era. The site features reconstructed buildings, costumed interpreters, and interactive exhibits that showcase the daily life of the fortress's inhabitants. Visitors can explore the fortress's ramparts, watch live demonstrations of traditional skills, and participate in hands-on activities.

Alexander Graham Bell National Historic Site:

The Alexander Graham Bell National Historic Site is a museum dedicated to the life and work of the famous inventor. The site features exhibits that showcase Bell's inventions, including the telephone and the hydrofoil boat. Visitors can also explore Bell's laboratory, which has been recreated to look as it did when he worked there.

Celtic Music Interpretive Centre:

The Celtic Music Interpretive Centre is a cultural center that showcases the rich music and dance traditions of Cape Breton Island. The center features exhibits that explore the history of Celtic music in Cape Breton, as well as live performances by local musicians and dancers. Visitors can also take workshops on traditional music and dance.

Whale watching tours:

Cape Breton Island is home to a variety of marine life, including whales, dolphins, and seals. Several companies offer whale watching tours that take visitors out into the ocean to see these animals in their natural habitat. Depending on the time of year, visitors may see humpback whales, minke whales, or fin whales. The tours also offer the opportunity to see seabirds and other marine life.

Overall, Cape Breton Island offers a variety of attractions that showcase its natural beauty, cultural richness, and outdoor activities. Whether you're interested in hiking, history, or music, there's something for everyone on this island.

Day trips from Cape Breton Island

Sydney:
Located on the eastern side of Cape Breton Island, Sydney is the largest city on the Island and offers a variety of attractions and activities. Some popular things to do in Sydney include:

- Visit the Cape Breton Centre for Craft and Design: This center showcases the work of local artists and craftsmen, including pottery, jewelry, and textiles.
- Explore the Jost House Museum: This museum is dedicated to the history of Sydney and showcases artifacts from the 18th and 19th centuries.
- Visit the Joan Harriss Cruise Pavilion: This pavilion is a popular destination for cruise ships and offers shopping, dining, and entertainment options.
- Take a walk along the Sydney Boardwalk: This boardwalk is a scenic path along the waterfront that offers stunning views of the harbor.

Baddeck:

Located on the shores of Bras d'Or Lake, Baddeck is a charming town with a rich history and outdoor activities. Some popular things to do in Baddeck include:

- Visit the Alexander Graham Bell National Historic Site: This museum is dedicated to the life and work of the famous inventor and features interactive exhibits and artifacts.
- Explore the Bras d'Or Lake Biosphere Reserve: This reserve is a UNESCO-designated biosphere that offers hiking trails, birdwatching, and kayaking.
- Visit the Uisage Ban Falls Provincial Park: This park features a scenic waterfall, hiking trails, and picnic areas.
- Take a boat tour of Bras d'Or Lake: Several companies offer boat tours of the lake, including fishing trips, sightseeing tours, and sunset cruises.

Louisbourg:

Located on the eastern side of Cape Breton Island, Louisbourg is a historic fishing village that showcases the way of life in colonial times. Some popular things to do in Louisbourg include:

- Visit the Fortress of Louisbourg National Historic Site: This site is a restored 18th-

century fortress that showcases life in the colonial era.
- Explore the Louisbourg Lighthouse: This lighthouse is a historic landmark that offers stunning views of the ocean and coastline.
- Visit the Louisbourg Playhouse: This theater offers a variety of performances, including plays, musicals, and concerts.
- Take a guided tour of the town: Several companies offer guided tours of Louisbourg, including walking tours and carriage rides.

Overall, there are plenty of day trips from Cape Breton Island that offer a variety of attractions and activities, from exploring historic sites to enjoying outdoor adventures.

Where to eat in Cape Breton Island

Cape Breton Island is known for its fresh seafood and unique cuisine that reflects its cultural heritage. Here are some of the best places to eat on the Island:

Lobster Pound and Moore: Located in North Sydney, this restaurant offers a wide selection of fresh seafood, including lobster, scallops, and fish and chips. They also have a variety of burgers and sandwiches for those who prefer land-based options.

The Chowder House: Situated in Baddeck, this restaurant serves delicious seafood chowder and other seafood dishes, including fish and chips, lobster rolls, and steamed mussels. They also have vegetarian options and a selection of desserts.

The Dancing Goat Cafe & Bakery: Located in Margaree, this cozy cafe offers homemade baked goods, sandwiches, and salads made with locally sourced ingredients. They also have a variety of coffee and tea options, as well as outdoor seating with views of the Margaree River.

The Bite House: This award-winning restaurant is located in Baddeck and offers a unique culinary experience with a fixed menu that changes daily. They use local, seasonal ingredients to create innovative dishes that showcase the flavors of Cape Breton Island.

The Red Shoe Pub: Situated in Mabou, this family-owned pub offers traditional Cape Breton dishes, including fish cakes, meat pies, and oatcakes. They also have live music and a friendly, welcoming atmosphere.

The Lobster Trap Restaurant: Located in Chéticamp, this restaurant offers a wide selection of fresh seafood, including lobster, crab, and scallops. They also have a variety of meat and vegetarian options, as well as a selection of desserts and cocktails.

Overall, Cape Breton Island offers a diverse range of dining options that cater to all tastes and budgets. Whether you're looking for fresh seafood, traditional Cape Breton cuisine, or gourmet dining experiences, you're sure to find something that satisfies your appetite on the Island.

Chapter 6: Northumberland Shore and Eastern Shore

Overview of the Northumberland Shore and Eastern Shore

The Northumberland Shore and Eastern Shore regions of Nova Scotia are often overlooked by visitors, but they offer a unique and beautiful experience for those who take the time to explore them. The Northumberland Shore is situated on the Northumberland Strait and is home to picturesque towns like Pictou and New Glasgow. The Eastern Shore, on the other hand, is a rugged and wild area that stretches along the Atlantic coast and is known for its stunning natural beauty.

Visitors to the Northumberland Shore can explore the charming town of Pictou, which is often referred to as the "birthplace of New Scotland". The town is steeped in Scottish history and is home to the Hector Heritage Quay, where visitors can learn about the Scottish migration to the area. Pictou also offers a beautiful waterfront area, with a marina and historic buildings.

The Northumberland Shore is also home to Northumberland Provincial Park, which offers a beautiful sandy beach and camping facilities.

Visitors can take a dip in the ocean, go for a hike on one of the park's trails, or enjoy a picnic with a view of the Northumberland Strait.

The Eastern Shore, on the other hand, offers a rugged and wild experience for visitors. The area is home to many small fishing communities and is known for its beautiful beaches, rugged coastline, and natural beauty. Visitors can explore the Musquodoboit Trailway, which offers stunning views of the Musquodoboit River, or visit the Memory Lane Heritage Village to learn about life in a 1940s Nova Scotia village.

Overall, the Northumberland Shore and Eastern Shore regions of Nova Scotia offer a unique blend of history, culture, and natural beauty. Visitors can explore historic towns, relax on sandy beaches, and immerse themselves in the local culture through a variety of activities and attractions.

Things to see and do in the Northumberland Shore and Eastern Shore

Pictou: This charming town is known as the "Birthplace of New Scotland" and is steeped in Scottish history and culture. Visitors can explore the Hector Heritage Quay, which features a full-scale replica of the Hector, the ship that brought Scottish immigrants to the area in 1773. The museum offers interactive exhibits and guided tours that allow visitors to experience what life was like for these early settlers. The town's waterfront area is also a popular destination, with a beautiful marina, restaurants, and historic buildings.

Northumberland Provincial Park: This park is located on the Northumberland Strait and offers visitors a chance to relax on a beautiful sandy beach. The beach is a popular spot for swimming, sunbathing, and beachcombing. The park also offers a variety of hiking trails, including the Coastal Trail, which offers stunning views of the Northumberland Strait and the surrounding coastline.

Antigonish: This small university town is known for its vibrant arts and culture scene. Visitors can explore the Antigonish Heritage Museum, which features exhibits on the town's history and culture, or attend a performance at the Bauer Theatre, which hosts a variety of plays, concerts, and other cultural events throughout the year.

Cape George Point Lighthouse: This picturesque lighthouse is located on a rocky point overlooking the Northumberland Strait. The lighthouse offers stunning views of the surrounding coastline and is a popular spot for photographers. Visitors can explore the hiking trails in the area or enjoy a picnic with a view of the sea.

Sherbrooke Village: This living history museum offers visitors a chance to step back in time and experience life in a 19th-century Nova Scotia village. The village features over 25 restored buildings, including homes, shops, and a church, as well as costumed interpreters who bring the village to life with traditional crafts and trades.

Arisaig Provincial Park: This park is located on the Northumberland Strait and offers visitors a chance to relax on a beautiful sandy beach. The warm waters of the Strait are perfect for swimming, and the park also offers a variety of hiking trails and picnic areas. Visitors can also explore the nearby Arisaig Provincial Heritage Centre, which features exhibits on the area's Scottish and Mi'kmaq heritage.

Musquodoboit Harbour: This small community is located on the Eastern Shore and offers visitors a chance to explore the great outdoors. The Musquodoboit Trailway is a popular destination for hikers and cyclists, with over 40 kilometers of trails that wind through forests, fields, and along rivers. The Musquodoboit River is also a popular spot for fishing, kayaking, and canoeing. Visitors can also learn about life in a 1940s Nova Scotia village at the Memory Lane Heritage Village, which features over 20 restored buildings and costumed interpreters.

Day trips from the Northumberland Shore and Eastern Shore

Arisaig Provincial Park:
Arisaig Provincial Park is a beautiful park located on the Northumberland Strait. The park features a long sandy beach that is perfect for swimming, sunbathing, and beachcombing. Visitors can also explore the nearby Arisaig Provincial Heritage Centre, which offers a variety of exhibits and programs focused on the area's history and culture. The centre also features a gift shop where visitors can purchase locally made crafts and souvenirs.

Musquodoboit Harbour:
Musquodoboit Harbour is a small community located on the Eastern Shore. The area is known for its natural beauty and offers a variety of outdoor activities for visitors to enjoy. One of the most popular activities is hiking on the Musquodoboit Trailway, a 15-kilometre trail that winds its way through forests, wetlands, and farmland. The trailway is suitable for hikers of all skill levels and offers stunning views of the surrounding countryside.

Visitors to Musquodoboit Harbour can also go fishing or kayaking in the Musquodoboit River, which is home to a variety of fish species including salmon, trout, and bass. The river is also a popular spot for birdwatching, with several species of waterfowl and songbirds calling the area home.

Another popular attraction in the area is the Memory Lane Heritage Village, a living history museum that offers a glimpse into life in a 1940s Nova Scotia village. Visitors can explore historic buildings, interact with costumed interpreters, and learn about traditional crafts and trades such as blacksmithing and candle-making. The village also features a gift shop and a restaurant that serves up traditional Nova Scotian dishes made with locally sourced ingredients.

Tangier and Sherbrooke:
Tangier and Sherbrooke are two small communities located on the Eastern Shore of Nova Scotia. These communities are rich in history and offer a variety of attractions and activities for visitors.

One of the highlights of Tangier is the Tangier Lobster Company, which offers tours of their lobster pound and processing facility. Visitors can learn about the lobster fishing industry in Nova Scotia and even have the opportunity to participate in a lobster boil.

In Sherbrooke, visitors can explore the Sherbrooke Village, a living history museum that offers a glimpse into life in a 19th-century Nova Scotia village. The village features over 25 historic buildings, including a general store, a church, and a blacksmith shop. Visitors can interact with costumed interpreters who demonstrate traditional crafts and trades such as spinning, weaving, and woodworking.

Sherbrooke also offers a variety of outdoor activities, including hiking, kayaking, and fishing. The St. Mary's River is a popular spot for fishing, with several species of trout and salmon available for anglers. The area also features several hiking trails, including the Liscomb River Trail, which offers stunning views of the river and surrounding wilderness.

Finally, visitors to the area can also take a scenic drive along the Eastern Shore Marine Drive, which offers stunning views of the coastline and passes through several charming communities along the way.

Where to eat in the Northumberland Shore and Eastern Shore

The Northumberland Shore and Eastern Shore regions of Nova Scotia have a vibrant culinary scene that offers visitors a taste of the local flavors and ingredients. Here are a few recommended restaurants and pubs to check out:

1. The Harbourview Restaurant (Pictou): This seafood restaurant is situated right on the waterfront in Pictou and offers stunning views of the Pictou Harbour. The menu features a variety of fresh seafood dishes, including lobster, scallops, and haddock. The restaurant prides itself on sourcing its seafood from local fishermen, ensuring that every dish is made with the freshest ingredients. In addition to seafood, the menu also offers a selection of salads, sandwiches, and burgers. The restaurant has indoor and outdoor seating options, and is open for lunch and dinner.

2. The Rare Bird Pub (Antigonish): This cozy pub is located in the heart of the historic town of Antigonish and offers a variety of craft beers and pub fare made with locally sourced ingredients. The menu features classic pub dishes such as burgers, wings, and fish and chips, as well as more innovative options like a beet and goat cheese salad or a Korean fried chicken sandwich. The Rare Bird also hosts live music on select nights, making it a popular spot for locals and visitors alike.

3. The Henley House Pub & Restaurant (Sheet Harbour): This family-friendly restaurant is located on the Eastern Shore and offers a range of dishes

made with locally sourced ingredients. The menu features classic pub fare such as burgers and sandwiches, as well as more upscale options like seafood chowder and lobster risotto. The Henley House also has a kids' menu and a selection of vegetarian and gluten-free options. In addition to the food, the pub also has a wide selection of beers and spirits.

4. The Henley House Bakery & Cafe (Sheet Harbour): This bakery and cafe is located next door to The Henley House Pub & Restaurant and offers a variety of fresh-baked breads, pastries, and desserts. The cafe also serves coffee, tea, and light meals such as sandwiches and salads. Visitors can enjoy their treats in the cozy seating area or take them to go for a picnic on the nearby beach.

5. The Station House Restaurant (Musquodoboit Harbour): This restaurant is located in a restored train station in the charming town of Musquodoboit Harbour on the Eastern Shore. The menu features a variety of dishes made with local ingredients, including seafood, steak, and pasta. The restaurant also offers a selection of vegetarian and gluten-free options. In addition to the food, the Station House also has an extensive wine list and a selection of craft beers.

Overall, the Northumberland Shore and Eastern Shore regions of Nova Scotia offer a range of dining options that showcase the local flavors and ingredients. Visitors can enjoy fresh seafood, locally sourced meats and produce, and a variety of craft beers and spirits. With options ranging from cozy pubs to upscale restaurants, there's something for every taste and budget.

Chapter 7: Outdoor Adventures in Nova Scotia

Nova Scotia is home to some of the most breathtaking natural scenery in Canada, making it an ideal destination for outdoor enthusiasts. This chapter highlights some of the best outdoor activities and adventures to be had in Nova Scotia, from hiking and walking to beach activities and wildlife watching.

Hiking and walking trails

Nova Scotia is a hiker's paradise, with over 1000km of hiking and walking trails that offer stunning views of the province's rugged coastline, lush forests, and rolling hills. From easy strolls to challenging hikes, there is something for everyone.

Overview of Nova Scotia's hiking and walking trails: Nova Scotia's hiking and walking trails are maintained by Parks Canada, the Nova Scotia Department of Natural Resources, and various other organizations. The trails range in length and difficulty, with some being suitable for families with young children, while others are more challenging and require a good level of fitness.

Top hiking and walking trails in Nova Scotia:

Some of the most popular hiking and walking trails in Nova Scotia include the Cabot Trail, Skyline Trail, and the Coastal Trail. The Cabot Trail is a 298km scenic drive that winds through Cape Breton Island's Highlands National Park, offering stunning views of the coast and the Cape Breton Highlands. The Skyline Trail is a 7.5km loop trail that offers panoramic views of the Gulf of St. Lawrence and the Cape Breton Highlands. The Coastal Trail is a 60km trail that runs along Nova Scotia's Eastern Shore, offering breathtaking views of the coastline and the Atlantic Ocean.

Tips for hiking and walking in Nova Scotia:

Before embarking on a hike, it's important to check the weather conditions and the trail conditions. Many trails are closed during the winter months or after heavy rainfall. It's also important to wear appropriate clothing and footwear, including sturdy hiking boots or shoes, layers to protect against the weather, and a hat and sunscreen for sun protection. It's also recommended to bring plenty of water, snacks, and a first aid kit. Trail etiquette is also important, including staying on designated trails, packing out all trash, and respecting wildlife and other hikers.

In conclusion, Nova Scotia's hiking and walking trails offer a fantastic way to experience the province's natural beauty and get some exercise in the great outdoors. With so many trails to choose from, visitors are sure to find a trail that suits their interests and fitness level. By following the tips outlined in this section, visitors can ensure a safe and enjoyable hiking or walking experience in Nova Scotia.

Beaches and water activities

Nova Scotia boasts over 7,600 kilometers of coastline, providing ample opportunities for beach activities and water sports. Whether you're a seasoned surfer or a casual beachgoer, Nova Scotia has something for everyone. Here are some top beaches and water activities to check out during your trip:

Top Beaches in Nova Scotia

- Lawrencetown Beach: Located on the Eastern Shore, Lawrencetown Beach is a popular spot for surfing and bodyboarding. Its long stretch of sandy beach and rolling waves make it a great place to spend a day by the water.
- Martinique Beach: Situated on the South Shore, Martinique Beach is a pristine stretch of sand and sea. With calm waters and gentle waves, it's ideal for swimming and beachcombing.
- Rainbow Haven Beach: Just a short drive from Halifax, Rainbow Haven Beach is a

popular family-friendly spot with lifeguards on duty during the summer months. Its wide expanse of sand and shallow waters make it a great spot for picnicking and playing in the water.

Water Activities in Nova Scotia

- Surfing: With its rugged coastline and Atlantic swells, Nova Scotia is a popular destination for surfers of all levels. Some top surf spots include Lawrencetown Beach, Cow Bay, and Point Michaud Beach.
- Kayaking: Nova Scotia's many lakes, rivers, and coastlines make it an ideal place for kayaking. Some popular kayaking routes include the LaHave River, St. Mary's River, and Cape Chignecto Provincial Park.
- Stand-Up Paddleboarding (SUP): SUP is a fun and easy way to explore Nova Scotia's waterways. Some top SUP spots include Mahone Bay, Prospect Bay, and Halifax Harbour.

Tips for Beach and Water Activities in Nova Scotia

- Dress in layers: Nova Scotia's weather can be unpredictable, so it's best to be prepared for all types of conditions. Bring a wetsuit or rash

guard for water activities, and pack warm layers for after your swim or surf session.
- Check the tide schedule: Many of Nova Scotia's beaches experience significant tidal changes throughout the day, so be sure to check the tide schedule before planning your beach day.
- Be aware of rip currents: Nova Scotia's coastline can be prone to rip currents, which can be dangerous for swimmers and surfers. Be sure to check the water conditions and always swim or surf near a lifeguarded beach if possible.
- Respect wildlife: Nova Scotia's coastline is home to a variety of wildlife, including seals, whales, and seabirds. Be sure to give wildlife plenty of space and avoid disturbing their natural habitats.

With its stunning beaches and diverse water activities, Nova Scotia is a top destination for beach lovers and water sports enthusiasts. Whether you're looking to catch some waves, explore the coast by kayak, or simply relax on the sand, there's no shortage of options to choose from.

Whale watching and wildlife tours

Whale watching and wildlife tours are some of the most popular outdoor activities in Nova Scotia, offering visitors the opportunity to see some of the province's most fascinating wildlife up close. From whales and dolphins to seabirds and seals, Nova Scotia is home to a diverse range of marine life that can be seen on a whale watching or wildlife tour.

Nova Scotia's whale watching season runs from May to October, with the peak season typically from July to September. During this time, visitors can see a variety of whale species, including humpback whales, minke whales, and fin whales. Some tour operators also offer the chance to see dolphins and porpoises, as well as a range of seabirds such as puffins and gannets.

One of the best places to go whale watching in Nova Scotia is the Bay of Fundy, which is home to the highest tides in the world and a variety of marine life. Tour operators in the Bay of Fundy offer both whale watching and wildlife tours, with some tours also including the opportunity to see seals, eagles, and other coastal wildlife.

Other popular whale watching and wildlife tour locations in Nova Scotia include Brier Island, which is known for its abundance of whales and seabirds, and Cape Breton Island, which offers the chance to see whales and dolphins as well as moose and other wildlife.

When planning a whale watching or wildlife tour in Nova Scotia, it's important to choose a reputable tour operator that follows ethical guidelines for wildlife viewing. Tour operators should follow regulations set by the Canadian government and ensure that their tours do not disturb or harm wildlife in any way. Visitors should also be prepared for the weather and wear warm clothing, as temperatures can be chilly out on the water.

Overall, a whale watching or wildlife tour in Nova Scotia is an unforgettable experience that offers a glimpse into the province's rich marine life and natural beauty. With a range of tour operators and locations to choose from, visitors are sure to find a tour that suits their interests and schedule.

Golf courses and skiing

Nova Scotia offers visitors a variety of options for outdoor activities beyond hiking and water sports, including golf and skiing. The province boasts some of the most stunning golf courses and ski resorts in Canada, making it an ideal destination for those looking for a little adventure on their trip.

Golf Courses
Nova Scotia is home to over 70 golf courses, ranging from challenging courses designed by world-renowned architects to laid-back courses with stunning ocean views. Here are some of the top golf courses to check out in Nova Scotia:

- Cabot Links: Located in Inverness, Cape Breton, this course is consistently ranked as one of the best golf courses in Canada, offering a challenging links-style course with stunning ocean views.
- Highlands Links: Also located in Inverness, Cape Breton, this course is known for its dramatic scenery and challenging terrain. The course was designed by famed golf course architect Stanley Thompson and features views of the ocean and surrounding mountains.
- Bell Bay Golf Club: Located in Baddeck, Cape Breton, this course offers stunning views of Bras d'Or Lake and the surrounding countryside. The course is known for its challenging layout and well-manicured greens.
- The Links at Brunello: Located just outside Halifax, this course offers a challenging layout with stunning views of the surrounding wilderness. The course features a mix of traditional and modern design elements, making it a unique golfing experience.

Skiing

While Nova Scotia may not be the first place that comes to mind when thinking of skiing destinations, the province offers some great ski hills and resorts for those looking to hit the slopes. Here are some of the top ski resorts to check out in Nova Scotia:

- Ski Wentworth: Located in Wentworth Valley, this resort offers a variety of runs for skiers of all levels, including a terrain park for snowboarders. The resort also offers snowshoeing and cross-country skiing trails.

- Martock Ski Hill: Located in Windsor, this ski hill offers a variety of runs for skiers and snowboarders, including a terrain park for advanced riders. The hill also offers night skiing and snowshoeing trails.

- Ski Cape Smokey: Located in Ingonish, Cape Breton, this ski hill offers stunning views of the ocean and surrounding mountains. The hill offers a variety of runs for skiers and snowboarders, as well as a terrain park and snow tubing park.

Overall, Nova Scotia offers a diverse range of outdoor activities beyond hiking and water sports, including golf and skiing. Visitors will find a variety of stunning courses and ski hills to explore, making it an ideal destination for those looking to add some adventure to their trip.

Chapter 8: Nova Scotia's Cultural Scene

Museums and historic sites

Nova Scotia has a fascinating history, and its museums and historic sites offer a glimpse into the province's past. Visitors can explore everything from military fortresses to shipwrecks to the home of an inventor. Here are some additional details on some of the top museums and historic sites in Nova Scotia:

- Halifax Citadel National Historic Site: This impressive fortress was built in the mid-18th century to protect Halifax from potential attacks. Today, visitors can tour the site and learn about its history through exhibits, guided tours, and interactive experiences. You can also see the Changing of the Guard ceremony during the summer months.

- Fortress of Louisbourg National Historic Site: This reconstructed French fortress on Cape Breton Island takes visitors back in time to the mid-18th century. Actors in period costumes bring the site to life, demonstrating everything from cooking and crafts to military drills. Visitors can also explore the buildings and gardens on their own and even participate in a musket firing demonstration.

- Maritime Museum of the Atlantic: Located in Halifax, this museum explores the history of Nova Scotia's relationship with the sea. Exhibits cover everything from shipwrecks and pirates to ocean liners and the Titanic. Visitors can also explore a collection of small boats and visit the museum's restored 1903 steamship, CSS Acadia.

- Alexander Graham Bell National Historic Site: This museum in Baddeck, on Cape Breton Island, celebrates the life and work of Alexander Graham Bell, inventor of the telephone. Visitors can tour the house where Bell lived and worked, see some of his inventions and artifacts, and learn about his other interests, including aviation and genetics.

  - Grand-Pré National Historic Site: This site in the Annapolis Valley commemorates the deportation of the Acadian people in the 18th century. Visitors can tour the museum and learn about the history of the Acadian people, their struggles, and their culture. The site also includes a beautiful park with walking trails and stunning views of the surrounding countryside.

These are just a few examples of the many museums and historic sites that Nova Scotia has to offer. Whether you're interested in military history, maritime history, or the history of the province's diverse cultural communities, there's sure to be a site that will fascinate you.

Festivals and events

Nova Scotia is a province that loves to celebrate, and there are many festivals and events that take place throughout the year. These events showcase the best of the province's culture, including its music, food, and heritage. Here are some of the top festivals and events that you won't want to miss during your visit to Nova Scotia:

Halifax International Busker Festival: This is one of the most popular festivals in the province, and it takes place in Halifax every August. The festival features street performers from all over the world, including acrobats, magicians, and comedians. There are also food vendors and live music performances to enjoy.

Celtic Colours International Festival: This festival celebrates the Celtic culture of Nova Scotia and takes place in October. It features concerts and workshops by local and international musicians, as well as events that showcase the province's Gaelic heritage. The festival takes place in various locations throughout Cape Breton Island, and it's a great way to experience the island's unique culture.

Halifax Pop Explosion: This music festival takes place in October and features indie and alternative music. It's a great way to discover new bands and see some of your favorites in an intimate venue. The festival takes place in various venues throughout Halifax, and there are often events that take place during the day as well as at night.

Nova Scotia Multicultural Festival: This festival celebrates the diversity of the province and takes place in June. It features food vendors, cultural performances, and activities for all ages. The festival is a great way to experience the different cultures that call Nova Scotia home, from African drumming to Celtic dancing.

Annapolis Valley Apple Blossom Festival: This festival takes place in May and celebrates the start of apple blossom season in the Annapolis Valley. There are parades, street fairs, and a coronation ceremony to crown the queen of the festival. The festival is a great way to experience the beauty of the valley and its famous apple orchards.

Halifax Jazz Festival: This summer music festival takes place in July and features jazz, blues, and world music. It takes place in various venues throughout Halifax, including indoor theaters and outdoor stages. The festival is a great way to experience the vibrant music scene in the city and discover new artists.

Halifax Seaport Beerfest: This event takes place in August and celebrates craft beer from all over North America. The festival features over 300 beers from more than 100 breweries, as well as food vendors and live music performances. It's a great way to discover new craft beers and enjoy a fun atmosphere with friends.

Halifax Pride Festival: This festival takes place in July and celebrates the LGBTQ+ community in Halifax. It features a parade, live performances, and events throughout the city. The festival is a great way to show support for the LGBTQ+ community and enjoy a fun and inclusive atmosphere.

Lunenburg Folk Harbour Festival: This music festival takes place in August and celebrates the traditional music of the Maritimes. It features concerts and workshops by local and international musicians, as well as events that showcase the province's maritime heritage. The festival takes place in the historic town of Lunenburg, which is a UNESCO World Heritage site and a beautiful place to visit.

Halifax International Film Festival: This film festival takes place in September and showcases films from all over the world. It's a great way to discover new films and support independent filmmakers. The festival takes place in various venues throughout Halifax, and there are often events and workshops that accompany the screenings.

Nova Scotia Lobster Crawl: This event takes place in February and celebrates Nova Scotia's famous lobster industry. It features lobster-themed events and experiences, such as lobster dinners, cooking classes, and lobster fishing tours. It's a great way to enjoy fresh seafood and learn about the province's fishing culture.

Halifax Oyster Festival: This festival takes place in October and celebrates Nova Scotia's oyster industry. It features oyster tastings, live music performances, and seafood vendors. The festival is a great way to enjoy fresh oysters and learn about the province's seafood industry.

These are just a few more examples of the many festivals and events that take place in Nova Scotia throughout the year. Whether you're interested in music, food, or culture, there is sure to be an event that you'll enjoy during your visit to the province.

Performing arts and music

Nova Scotia has a vibrant performing arts scene, with many theaters, concert halls, and music venues showcasing local and international talent. Here are some of the top performing arts and music venues in the province:

Neptune Theatre: Established in 1963, Neptune Theatre is the largest professional theater company in Atlantic Canada. Located in Halifax, the theater produces a wide range of plays and musicals throughout the year, featuring local and international talent. The theater has two stages, the Fountain Hall and the Scotiabank Stage, and also offers theater classes and workshops.

Rebecca Cohn Auditorium: Located on the campus of Dalhousie University in Halifax, the Rebecca Cohn Auditorium is a 1,000-seat concert hall that hosts a wide range of musical performances, from classical to contemporary. The auditorium is home to Symphony Nova Scotia, the province's professional orchestra, and also hosts touring musicians and performers.

Halifax Jazz Festival: The Halifax Jazz Festival is an annual music festival that takes place in downtown Halifax. Established in 1987, the festival features jazz, blues, and world music, and attracts thousands of visitors each year. The festival takes place over several days in July, with performances at various venues throughout the city.

Symphony Nova Scotia: Symphony Nova Scotia is the province's professional orchestra, and performs a wide range of classical and contemporary music throughout the year. The orchestra has a home base at the Rebecca Cohn Auditorium in Halifax, and also performs in other venues throughout the province. Symphony Nova Scotia also offers educational programs for children and adults.

Halifax Pop Explosion: The Halifax Pop Explosion is a music festival that takes place in downtown Halifax in October. The festival features indie and alternative music, with performances at various venues throughout the city. The festival also includes a conference component, with industry panels and workshops.

Mermaid Theatre of Nova Scotia: Founded in 1972, Mermaid Theatre of Nova Scotia is a touring theater company that specializes in puppetry and storytelling. The company has performed throughout Canada and around the world, and is based in Windsor, Nova Scotia. Mermaid Theatre of Nova Scotia is especially known for its adaptations of classic children's books, such as The Very Hungry Caterpillar and Goodnight Moon.

Nova Scotia's performing arts and music scene is diverse and lively, with many talented local and international performers. Whether you're interested in theater, classical music, jazz, or indie rock, you're sure to find something to enjoy during your visit to Nova Scotia.

Art galleries and studios

Nova Scotia has a thriving arts community, and there are many galleries and studios where you can view and purchase artwork created by local artists. The province is particularly known for its folk art, which is characterized by its whimsical, brightly colored designs and use of recycled materials.

The Art Gallery of Nova Scotia is the largest art museum in the province and is a must-visit destination for art lovers. The museum's collection includes more than 17,000 works by local and international artists, including paintings, sculptures, and photographs. The museum also hosts temporary exhibitions throughout the year that showcase the work of emerging and established artists.

The Mary E. Black Gallery is another great destination for art lovers. The gallery focuses on contemporary craft and design and features exhibitions by artists working in a range of mediums, including ceramics, textiles, and jewelry.

The gallery also hosts workshops and classes where you can learn more about different craft techniques.

In Cape Breton, the Cape Breton Centre for Craft and Design is a hub for traditional and contemporary craft. The center offers classes and workshops in a range of crafts, including pottery, weaving, and woodturning. The center also has a gallery where you can view and purchase handmade crafts created by local artisans.

In addition to these larger galleries and centers, Nova Scotia has many smaller galleries and studios that showcase the work of local artists. The Artisans Gallery in Halifax, for example, features the work of more than 30 artists working in a range of mediums, including ceramics, glass, and wood. The Teichert Gallery in Halifax also showcases the work of local artists and hosts regular exhibitions throughout the year.

If you're interested in seeing artists at work, there are many studios in Nova Scotia that offer tours and demonstrations. The Lunenburg Art Gallery in Lunenburg, for example, has a studio where you can watch artists at work and learn more about their craft. The Cape Breton Centre for Craft and Design also offers tours of its studio spaces.

Nova Scotia's art galleries and studios are a testament to the province's vibrant arts community.

Whether you're interested in traditional crafts or contemporary art, you'll find plenty to enjoy during your visit. Be sure to check out the events calendar to see what exhibitions and events are happening during your stay. And don't forget to pick up a piece of locally made art as a souvenir of your trip.

Chapter 9: Practical Information

Nova Scotia's history and culture

Nova Scotia's history and culture:
Nova Scotia is a province with a rich and complex history, shaped by its geography, Indigenous heritage, and various waves of immigration. The region was first inhabited by Indigenous peoples, including the Mi'kmaq, who have lived in the area for thousands of years. The province was later colonized by the French in the 17th century, and then by the British in the 18th century, leading to a mix of cultures and traditions that continue to shape the province today.

Key events and historical figures:

Nova Scotia has played an important role in Canadian and North American history, from its strategic location as a gateway to the Atlantic Ocean to its contributions to the country's economy and culture. Some of the key events and historical figures associated with Nova Scotia include the Halifax Explosion of 1917, the Acadian Expulsion of 1755, the Scottish immigration in the 18th century, and the role of Halifax as a key port city during World War II. Famous historical figures associated with Nova Scotia include Samuel Cunard, who founded the Cunard shipping line, and Anne Murray, a singer-songwriter who achieved international success in the 1970s and 80s.

Indigenous culture and heritage:
The Indigenous peoples of Nova Scotia, particularly the Mi'kmaq, have a rich and vibrant culture that has been passed down for generations. Visitors to the province can learn about this culture through museums, cultural centers, and tours led by Indigenous guides. Key aspects of Mi'kmaq culture include storytelling, drumming and singing, and traditional arts and crafts such as basket weaving.

Acadian culture and heritage:

The Acadians were a French-speaking population who settled in Nova Scotia in the 17th and 18th centuries. Their culture and traditions continue to be celebrated in the province through festivals, museums, and historic sites. Visitors can learn about Acadian music, food, and crafts, as well as their history and struggles during the Acadian Expulsion.

Scottish culture and heritage:

Nova Scotia has a strong Scottish heritage, dating back to the arrival of Scottish immigrants in the 18th century. Scottish culture is celebrated through festivals, music, and dance, as well as through the many Scottish place names in the province. Visitors can learn about Scottish traditions such as tartan weaving, Highland games, and the playing of bagpipes.

In conclusion, Nova Scotia's history and culture are integral parts of the province's identity and offer visitors a unique and fascinating glimpse into the region's past and present. By learning about the Indigenous, Acadian, and Scottish cultures of the province, visitors can gain a deeper appreciation for the diversity and complexity of Nova Scotia's heritage.

Money and costs

Currency and exchange rates
The official currency in Nova Scotia is the Canadian dollar. Visitors can exchange their currency at banks, currency exchange booths, and some hotels. It's advisable to check the exchange rate before exchanging money to avoid getting ripped off. Major credit cards such as Visa, Mastercard, and American Express are widely accepted in Nova Scotia, and there are ATMs available in most towns and cities.

Cost of travel in Nova Scotia

The cost of travel in Nova Scotia varies depending on the season, the type of accommodation, and the activities you want to do. Generally, summer is the peak season, and prices for accommodations and activities can be higher during this time. Budget travelers can find affordable accommodations in hostels, guesthouses, and budget hotels, while luxury travelers can enjoy high-end hotels and resorts. Some activities like hiking and exploring beaches are free, while others like whale watching and golfing can be more expensive.

Budget tips and advice

- To save money on your trip to Nova Scotia, consider some of these budget tips:
- Travel off-season: Prices for accommodations and activities can be much lower during the off-season.
- Cook your meals: Rent a vacation home or stay in a hostel with a kitchen and cook your meals instead of eating out.
- Use public transportation: Instead of renting a car, use public transportation like buses and ferries to get around.
- Look for deals: Check websites like Groupon and Travelzoo for deals on accommodations and activities.

Payment options and credit cards

Credit cards are widely accepted in Nova Scotia, but it's advisable to carry some cash for smaller transactions. ATMs are available in most towns and cities, and many banks have branches that are open on weekends. It's a good idea to inform your bank that you'll be traveling to Canada to avoid any issues with your credit card.

Tipping etiquette

In Nova Scotia, it's customary to tip around 15-20% in restaurants and bars if the service was good. It's also common to tip hotel staff, taxi drivers, and tour guides around 10-15% if you were satisfied with their service. Tipping is not mandatory, but it's a good way to show appreciation for good service.

Health and safety

Nova Scotia is generally a safe and healthy destination for travelers, but it's always wise to take some precautions to ensure your trip goes smoothly. Here are some key things to keep in mind:

Vaccinations and Health Precautions:

- No specific vaccinations are required to enter Nova Scotia.

- It's always a good idea to be up to date on routine vaccinations, such as measles, mumps, rubella, and tetanus.
- Travelers should take precautions against ticks and mosquitoes, particularly during the summer months.
- Tick-borne diseases such as Lyme disease are present in Nova Scotia, so it's important to wear protective clothing, use insect repellent, and check your body for ticks after spending time outdoors.
- It's also important to be aware of the potential for waterborne illnesses, particularly in lakes and rivers. Drinking water from untreated sources can lead to illness, so be sure to either bring your own water or treat water before consuming it.

Medical Services and Facilities:

- Medical services in Nova Scotia are generally of a high standard.
- In case of emergency, dial 911 for assistance.
- There are hospitals and clinics throughout the province, and medical care is generally covered by the provincial health insurance plan for Canadian residents.
- However, non-residents may be required to pay for medical services, so it's important to have travel insurance that covers medical expenses.

- Pharmacies are widely available throughout Nova Scotia and can provide over-the-counter medications as well as prescription drugs.

Emergency Contacts:

- In case of emergency, dial 911 for police, fire, or medical assistance.
- The non-emergency number for the police is 902-490-5016.
- The non-emergency number for the fire department is 902-490-5530.
- The non-emergency number for ambulance services is 902-865-3666.

Safety Tips for Outdoor Activities:

- Nova Scotia is known for its rugged coastline and beautiful natural areas, but these areas can also pose some risks.
- When hiking, always stay on marked trails and carry appropriate safety gear, such as a map, compass, and flashlight.
- Swimming in the ocean can be dangerous due to strong currents and cold temperatures, so it's important to be aware of the conditions and only swim in designated areas.
- When boating, always wear a lifejacket and follow all safety regulations.
- Be aware of the potential for wildlife encounters, particularly with black bears and

moose. It's important to keep a safe distance and never approach or feed wild animals.

Crime and Security in Nova Scotia:

- Nova Scotia is generally a safe destination for travelers, but it's always wise to take some basic precautions to ensure your safety.
- Petty theft, such as pickpocketing and purse-snatching, can occur in tourist areas and crowded places, so it's important to be aware of your surroundings and keep valuables secure.
- Violent crime is rare in Nova Scotia, but it's still important to exercise caution, particularly at night or in isolated areas.
- The emergency number for the police is 911.

Language and communication

Official languages in Nova Scotia:

Nova Scotia's official languages are English and French. English is the most widely spoken language, with French being spoken predominantly in the Acadian regions of the province.

Common phrases and expressions:

When traveling to Nova Scotia, it can be helpful to learn some common phrases and expressions in English and French. Here are some examples:

English:
Hello / Hi - "How are you?"
Thank you - "You're welcome."
Please - "Excuse me."
Goodbye - "See you later."

French:

Bonjour / Salut - "Comment ça va?"
Merci - "De rien."
S'il vous plaît - "Pardon."
Au revoir - "À bientôt."

Translation and interpretation services:

If you need translation or interpretation services during your trip, there are several resources available. Many hotels and tourist centers offer multilingual services, and there are also professional translation and interpretation companies that you can hire. Additionally, there are online translation tools that can help you communicate with locals.

Internet and communication services:

Nova Scotia has reliable internet and communication services, including Wi-Fi hotspots and mobile networks. Most hotels, restaurants, and cafes offer free Wi-Fi, and you can purchase a prepaid SIM card or a mobile plan from one of the province's major telecommunications companies.

Tips for communicating with locals:

To ensure smooth communication with locals, it's important to be polite, respectful, and patient. Here are some tips to keep in mind:

- Speak slowly and clearly, especially if you have a strong accent.
- Avoid using slang or jargon that might be unfamiliar to locals.
- Be mindful of cultural differences and customs, such as greetings and body language.
- Use gestures and visuals if necessary to help convey your message.
- Always say "please" and "thank you" to show appreciation.

By keeping these tips in mind and being respectful of local customs, you'll be able to communicate effectively and enjoyably during your trip to Nova Scotia.

Useful apps and websites

When traveling to Nova Scotia, there are many useful apps and websites that can help you plan your trip and make the most of your time in the province. Here are some examples:

Tourism Nova Scotia: This is the official tourism website for Nova Scotia, where you can find information on accommodations, attractions, events, and more. The website also offers a trip planning tool and a blog with travel tips and inspiration.

Nova Scotia Tides: This app provides real-time tide information for more than 200 locations along the Nova Scotia coast. It's especially useful for beachcombing, fishing, and other coastal activities.

Nova Scotia Liquor Corporation (NSLC): This app allows you to browse and purchase wine, beer, and spirits from NSLC stores across the province. You can also create a wishlist, track your purchases, and find store locations.

Google Maps: This app is a must-have for any traveler, as it provides maps, directions, and real-time traffic information. You can also use it to search for restaurants, attractions, and other points of interest.

Weather Network: This app provides up-to-date weather forecasts and alerts for Nova Scotia, including temperature, precipitation, and wind conditions. It's especially useful for planning outdoor activities.

CBC News: This app provides local and national news coverage, including breaking news, weather, and sports. It's a great way to stay informed about current events in Nova Scotia.

GasBuddy: This app helps you find the cheapest gas prices in your area, which can save you money on your road trip around Nova Scotia.

Roadtrippers: This app is perfect for planning a road trip in Nova Scotia. You can use it to find interesting stops and attractions along your route, as well as hotels, restaurants, and other amenities.

Airbnb: This app allows you to search for and book unique accommodations in Nova Scotia, including apartments, cottages, and even lighthouses. You can also connect with local hosts who can provide insider tips and recommendations.

HappyCow: This app is a must-have for vegetarians and vegans traveling to Nova Scotia. It provides a directory of vegetarian and vegan restaurants, as well as health food stores and other plant-based businesses.

AllTrails: This app is perfect for hikers and outdoor enthusiasts, as it provides detailed trail maps, reviews, and photos for hiking, biking, and other outdoor activities in Nova Scotia.

Nova Scotia Beaches: This app provides information on more than 100 beaches in Nova Scotia, including water quality, amenities, and accessibility. It's a great resource for beachgoers and surfers.

Parks Canada: This app provides information on national parks and historic sites in Nova Scotia, including admission fees, hours of operation, and events. You can also use it to purchase passes and reserve campsites.

TripIt: This app is a travel organizer that helps you keep track of your itinerary, flights, hotels, and other reservations. It's especially useful for longer trips with multiple destinations.

By using these apps and websites, you can streamline your trip planning and make the most of your time in Nova Scotia. Whether you're looking for a unique accommodation, a great restaurant, or a scenic hiking trail, these tools can help you find what you're looking for.

Conclusion

In conclusion, the Nova Scotia Travel Guide is your ultimate companion to exploring this beautiful province. With its rugged coastline, charming small towns, and fascinating history, Nova Scotia has something to offer every traveler.

Through this guidebook, we have provided you with insider tips and local recommendations to help you discover the best of Nova Scotia. From the vibrant city of Halifax to the breathtaking scenery of Cape Breton Island, you'll find detailed information on where to stay, what to see and do, and where to eat.

Whether you're seeking outdoor adventures, cultural experiences, or a relaxing retreat, this guide has got you covered. Our comprehensive coverage of Nova Scotia's hiking trails, beaches, museums, and festivals will help you make the most of your time in this remarkable province.

We hope this guide has inspired you to embark on an unforgettable journey through Nova Scotia. As you explore this region's natural beauty and rich cultural heritage, we are confident that you will fall in love with Nova Scotia, just as we have.

So pack your bags, grab this guide, and get ready to discover the best of Nova Scotia. We can't wait to hear about your adventures and experiences in this beautiful province.

Made in United States
North Haven, CT
16 March 2023

34179848R00083